KARUNAMIRTHA SAGARAM

KARUNAMIRTHA SAGARAM

RAO SAHIB M. ABRAHAM PANDITHER

EXTRACT
FROM
THE FIRST BOOK
ON
SRUTIS

PART I, II, & III

An essay on Srutis read before the All-India Music Conference held at Baroda under the kind patronage of His Highness the Gaekwar of Baroda ((22nd March, 1916)

GYAN

Published by

GYAN

Gyan Publishing House
5, Ansari Road
Daryaganj, New Delhi-110002
Phone: 011-47034999, 9811692060
E-mail: books@gyanbooks.com

Distribution Network
gyanbooks.com
India, USA, Canada, UK, Australia, France

ISBN : 978-81-212-9921-3 (PB)
First Published, 1917

2nd Impression 2021

Printed at: Gyan Press, Delhi.

KARUNAMIRTHA SAGARAM
Author: RAO SAHIB M. ABRAHAM PANDITHER

KARUNAMIRTHA SAGARAM.

RAO SAHIB M. ABRAHAM PANDITHER

EXTRACT FROM THE FIRST BOOK ON SRUTIS

PART I, II & III

An essay on Srutis read before the All-India Music Conference held at Baroda under the kind patronage of His Highness the Gaekwar of Baroda (22nd March, 1916)

KARUNAMIRTHA SAGARAM.

EXTRACT FROM THE FIRST BOOK ON SRUTIS.

An essay on Srutis read before the All-India Music Conference held at Baroda under the kind patronage of His Highness the Gaekwar of Baroda (March 1916).

INTRODUCTION.

YOUR Highness the Gaekwar who is ever anxious to introduce reforms for the improvement of the different fine arts and handicrafts and the learned members of this august body who are assembled here with a deep interest for the advancement of Indian music! we considered hitherto the correct method of arriving at the Dwavimsati Srutis of Sarnga Dev who flourished at the beginning of the 13th century. In the same manner, I think it will clear the doubt overhanging the Srutis, if we could also consider the opinion on Srutis given by Ilankovadigal, who lived at the commencement of the 1st century, in his work Silappadikaram.

The Srutis of South Indian Music according to Isai-Tamil.

(Karunamirtha Sagaram in Tamil Page 517 — 522.)

We have noted before, that the music of the renowned ancient India was in the highest state of efficiency at one time, and that when it began to deteriorate, the scientific works of the period also were despised on the score of impracticability when compared with modern requirements.

We have also noted in the Tables given above, that though many writers have taken the greatest pains to interpret ancient musical works correctly and restore them to their original eminence, yet they have not determined the Srutis after the system of Sarnga Dev but according to their own fancy.

We hold with pardonable pride that all the fine arts—Music, Painting, Poetry, Sculpture and Architecture—flourished scientifically in India from very ancient times and that each of them had advanced to such an extent so as to possess well established rules. In support of this we see, even at the present day, colossal buildings of rare architectural beauty, temples, beautiful pictures, life-like statues in granite, exquisitely moulded figures in different metals, ancient poems which delight the hearers to a remarkable degree and any number of Ragas to chant these poems in a melodious manner.

Just as a tailor is able to make a man's coat when the measurement of his necl alone is given, our ancestors were able to cut out the figure of a man from granite or mould his figure with only the dimensions of the little finger for a clue. They were able to make the figure of a woman, with the help of her hair, which went floating along in water, its length and thickness alone being known. In proportion to this advanced knowledge thay had some measurements in each science which exist even at the present day.

On the other hand, we find from experience that the measurements of Srutis which form the basis of all music (the best of fine arts) and the system of producing Ragas from Srutis, have gone out of use for many years. Fortunately, these Srutis, the Ragas based upon those Srutis, and the compositions of our ancestors have been preserved by traditional and oral transmission. We have to regret that the music of those who are ignorant of Srutis and the Ragas derived from them is as useless as the linguistic ability of a man who has learnt many languages just by hearing them talked, without being able to read or write any of them.

Many scholars have worked in this important field for years and have published their experience and the resutt of their researches in the form of books. Hoping that some of the distinguished Karnatic musicians would help in arriving at definite conclusions as regards Srutis, the Sangeetha Vidhya Mahajana Sangam was started by me in Tanjore on the 27th of May 1912. We have had six conferences till now and many different opinions have been given as regards Srutis. This led me to give my own views on the subject. I sincerely believe that my system of Srutis is flawless I also presume, like the great writers that have gone before me, that my system would clear the doubts of all Indians. I beg that this presumption of mine, will be pardoned by the scholars present in this assembly as well as by His Highness the Gaekwar, v versed in all arts and sciences.

"Karunamirtha Sagaram" is the name of my book treating on Srutis; 872 pages of this book have been already printed and only a few more pages remain. Of the 512 pages have been already translated into English and printed. Though my work is still incomplete, as I received orders that I should say something about Srutis before the "All-India music conference" and before H. H. the Gaekwar, I am compelled to reproduce a few points from my printed book.

Sarnga Dev has given his opinion about Srutis very clearly. We gather fron ancient Tamil works that Ilankovadigal has also written very lucidly on the subject. think we shall do well to examine the systems of the above two writers.

I sincerely thank your Highness as well as the learned scholars who have assembled here for the purpose of arriving at truth and establishing it at any cost.

The system of Dwavimsati Srutis according to Sarnga Dev, the author of Sangeetha Ratnakaram, and the opinions of different writers who determine the Dwavimsati Srutis in an octave by taking Sa-Pa as 2/3.

President and Members of this Conference,

It seems that from the time of Pythagoras, the Greek philosopher, who visited India about 2500 years ago for purposes of obtaining information, the system of determining the Swarams of an octave by the principle of SA-PA $\frac{2}{3}$ and Sa-Ma $\frac{3}{4}$ began. We know that the Sthayi never comes to a perfect end while adopting either of the measurements. The fact that the series of Swarams obtained by the principle of $\frac{2}{3}$ (Sa-Pa) extend a little beyond the octave, while the series obtained by Sa-Ma or $\frac{3}{4}$ fall a little short of the octave, was the cause of difference of opinion among the writers as regards Swarasthanams. Many writers in India have written treatises as regards the theories of Swarasthanams which they have arrived at after strenuous labour. The works of Bharata (V Century A. D.) who is looked upon as the pioneer of music and that of Sarnga Dev (author of Sangeeta Ratnakaram) are held in very high esteem at the present day as standard works on Indian Music. The above two writers speak of 22 Srutis in the octave. But they never give the measurements Sa-Pa $\frac{2}{3}$ and Sa-Ma $\frac{3}{4}$. They derive 13 Srutis by the Sa-Pa series and 9 by the Sa-Ma series and claim the relationship of Vadi and Samvadi for these Swarams. Moreover, Sarnga Dev gives a few directions as to how these Srutis of an octave should be derived. Speaking about the progression of sound in the Sthayis, he says that the one of Mandara Sthayi becomes two in Madhya Sthayi and four in the Thara Sthayi thus gradually proceeding upwards in a particular ratio. As regards Srutis he says that the 22 Srutis of an octave are a gradually ascending series with a uniform ratio without admitting any other possible sound between. Then as regards change of Graham he says that when out of the four Srutis of Sa two are lessened, the Ga and Ni become Ri and Dha and when three Srutis are lessened, the Ri and Dha become Sa and Pa. Putting all the above three directions together we see plainly that he derives the 22 Srutis in the octave by Geometrical Progression. I have given the mathematical calculations for the 22 Srutis in the octave, their position in a wire 32 inches long, the number of vibrations and the cents calculations. This is the only and right method by which Srutis can be derived in accordance with the Slokas of Sarnga Dev. The change of Graham can be made possible only if this method is adopted. No matter where we commence the Swarasthanams, the change of Graham will be possible only if the pitch of sounds be uniform according to Sarnga Dev. This clearly implies that the Srutis should be of equal intervals. On the other hand many give measurements of Srutis with unequal intervals quite contrary to that of Sarnga Dev, and try to palm them off as those of Sarnga Dev. There is not the slightest resemblance between the theory of Sarnga Dev and those of the writers on Swarams and Srutis of the modern day.

According to Sarnga Dev, PA or $\frac{3}{2}$ has 709 cents while according to others it has 702; the MA of Sarnga Dev has 491 cents while that of others has 498. If there is such a difference as regards the two fundamental Swarams MA and PA in music, either of the two opinions must be wrong. But we know that the Swarams MA and PA are $\frac{4}{3}$ and $\frac{3}{2}$ approximately. If there is a slight mistake in an opinion that has been commonly accepted, it is our duty to correct it and advance it instead of rejecting it altogether. If we notice the Swarams and Srutis of the Karnatic Ragas used in the beautiful Tamil country where music was fostered from ancient times, we may observe that the music was one which has had its excellent rules for thousands of years, that ,he Swarams SA-PA $\frac{3}{2}$ and SA-MA $\frac{4}{3}$ were known as Inai Swaram or Kalathira Swaram and Kilai Swaram or Putthra Swaram respectively and that the same relation of Swarams as Kalathira and Putthira are found in the fifth and the seventh Sthanams in Astrology. The doubt about the Dwavimsati Srutis found in the writings of Bharata, Sarnga Dev and other writers who make mention of the principle of $\frac{3}{2}$ and $\frac{4}{3}$ is completely dispelled by Silappadikaram, an ancient Tamil work written by Ilankovadigal (about 50. A. D.) which gives a few rules about Isai-Tamil. There we may see the 12 Swarams of Ayapalai derived by the SA-PA and the SA-MA systems. the 24 Alakus of Vattappalai where Ganam was made possible with two Alakus less, the different Yals of Vattapalai and the four Jathis derived from each of them and the measurements for the Srutis of Thirikonapalai and Chathurapalai. These will be clearly dealt with in the next essay.

The Sruti System of Sarnga Dev.

The Dwavimsati Srutis of Indian music according to Sangeetha Ratnakaram.

(Karunamirtha Sagaram in English p. 400 to 416)

Though many are of opinion that it is quite possible to determine the 22 Srutis in Indian music and to bring them to practical use, yet it seems to be a hopeless task owing to the conflicting opinions of the writers on the subject. Some of them have studied the Srutis of Hindustani music, and have given their opinion, while others pick out a line here and a line there from ancient authors and try to palm them off as their own. However, we will do well to point out the contradiction in their theories first and then speak about the Srutis in use in South Indian music. For, it is manifest from the writings of the above authors, that they merely adopted the term Dwavimsati Srutis of Sarnga Dev and marked the Swarasthanams without trying to understand his real meaning in the determination of Srutis. Some gave Tables of Srutis which applied only to Hindustani music, which resembled more or less the modes of the Western musicians. Others copied the same Western modes, altering only a few Swarams here and there, and called them the Srutis of South Indian music. But it makes one smile to think, that all these conflicting theories are palmed off as the Dwavimsati Srutis of Sarnga Dev.

The above writers merely made the term Dwavimsati Srutis the burden of their song without understanding the real meaning and dignity of Sangeeta Ratnakaram, and distributed the Srutis in the octave in any way they liked. It is clear that they have not grasped even an iota of the meaning of Sarnga Dev. It is impossible to reconcile an ancient and imparacticable theory with a modern one. The ancient works should be examined in the light of modern criticism, and all that is imparacticable should be given up and all that is good should be accepted. An ancient work may continue to be good even at the modern day, but it may also be superseded by a modern work owing to exigencies of time. It is the duty of wise men to discriminate between the two and hold fast that which is good. It is not advisable either to give up an ancient work which is good on the plea of its being imparacticable now; on the other hand, an ancient work which conflicts with the modern practicability must certainly be discouraged. We shall understand presently that the system of Sarnga Dev is alien to South Indian music, just as it does not suit the music of the north. We have to examine here the system of Sarnga Dev because Sangeeta Ratnakaram is held in high esteem as the standard work on Indian music. So we shall determine the Srutis according to his system and compare them with those of other writers who also swear by him, and then draw our own conclusions and not blindly grope about in the dark like the above writers.

The very fact that the octaves as they proceed should have the vibration of their Srutis in Geometrical Progression shows, that the music of the ancient days was highly efficient. Just as the octaves proceed in the ratio of 1, 2, 4, 8 etc., so also the Swarams should do, he says. This should be carefully noted. Many have erred because they did not note this. We might clear all our doubts if we examine the 22 Srutis mentioned in his book, how they stand when the Gramams are changed and how far they agree. The different opinions given by the various writers on the 22 Srutis, namely, Mr. Sahasrabuddhi, Mr. Raja Surendra Mohan Tagore, Mr. Devāl, Mr. Clements, Mr. Nagoji Row, Mr. Brave, Dr. Bhandarkar, Mr. Manicka Mudaliar who wrote Sangeeta Chandrika, Mr. Chinnasami Mudaliar, M. A., Mr. Subramania Sastrial, Mr. Panchapakesa Bhagavatar, Mr. Pratapa Ramasami Bhagavatar and others, made us conclude that the opinion of Sarnga Dev must be something different. The following Tables will show that the above writers who determined the Srutis, having his book as their authority, have gone clean out of his track as regards the Srutis. So we shall do well to find out the Srutis first according to his system, prove their correctness by seeing whether they stand the test of change of Gramam, and then compare them with the calculations of those who have interpreted him Then we shall come to the conclusion either that these are not Dwavimsati Srutis or that the author of Ratnakaram gives a completely different view.

The main idea of Sarnga Dev as regards Srutis given in his Chapter on Swarams is as follows:—

"An idea in the mind generates Agni, which in its turn generates Vayu. This Vayu proceeds upwards from the Brahmakranthi or Mooladharam through the stomach, the heart, the trunk, the head and the mouth in the shape of Nadam. In these five places, Nadam obtains the five corresponding names of Ati Sookshmam, Sookshmam, Pushtam, Apushtam and Krithrimum. The Nadam increases in intensity in the ratio of 1, 2 and 4 being Mandaram in the heart, Madhymam in the trunk and Taram in the head. The sound which is thus produced has 22 varieties. The sound which could be distinctly heard is called Sruti. There are two breathing apparatuses going upwards from the heart which are called Idaikalai and Pinkalai. There are 22 (Nadis) arterial passages across these 22. When the air passes through them these passages dilate and the sound comes out. In the same manner there are 22 Sthanams in the trunk and the head. This may be proved with the help of two Veenas.

Have two Veenas with 22 strings each. In the first Veena, tune one of the strings so as to produce the lowest possiple sound. Tune the second string so that it might sound the next possible note. No sound should be possible between the two. Arrange and tune all the wires on the same principle. Now the wires are arranged and tuned in a progressive series. Of these SA has 4 Srutis. Fix the 4th of these Srutis as the SA. RI will have 3 Srutis, or in other words the 5th, the 6th and the 7th strings will be the varieties of RI. The two Srutis of GA will stand on the 8th and 9th wires. The four Srutis of MA will be on the 10th, 11th, 12th and the 13th wires. The 14th, 15th, 16th and the 17th wires will sound the 4 Srutis of PA, while the 3 Srutis of DHA will occur on the next three strings. The last two strings of the Veena will be responsible for the two Srutis of NI. One of these Veenas is Dhruva Veena and the other Chala Veena. Alter the strings of the latter as directed below. If you arrange the seven Swarams commencing them from the 3rd Sruti of SA instead of the 4th, you will have one Sruti less. If you commence the series from the second Sruti of SA, GA and NI will obtain one of the Srutis of RI and DHA.

If three Srutis are left out, Ri and Dha will have the 4 Srutis of Sa and Pa. But when you commence the series leaving all the 4 Srutis of Sa on the left Ri, Ga, and Ma of Dhruva Veena will correspond with the Sa Ma and Pa of Chala Veena. In other words, Sa commences on the 22nd, Ma on the 9th and Pa on the 13th. By this means, the calculations of Srutis may be obtained. From these Srutis proceed the seven fundamental Swarams Sa, Ri, Ga, Ma, Pa, Dha, and Ni.

Sa is of two varieties—Suddha Sa and Atchyuta Sa. When you reduce the 4 Srutis of Sa into 3, Ri obtains 4 Srutis. In the same way when Ma is reduced by one of its Srutis, it becomes Suddha Ma. When two of the Srutis of Sa are absorbed into Kakali Ni, it is called Achyuta Sa. This is a Vikriti Swaram.

In the same way when Ma gives two of its Srutis to Anthara Ga and has only two Srutis, it is called Achuta Ma. This is also a Vikriti Sruti. When Sa, with one Sruti less, commences the 22nd Sthanam, the 23rd Sthanam is Kaisika and the 24th Kakali. Both these Swarams are Vikriti. The Sa which comes in the 3rd place after Kakali is Suddha Sa. This is also a Vikriti Swaram. Ma is likewise Vikriti. In the same manner when Ma has only two Srutis, it is called Achyuta Ma, which is also Vikriti. When Ma gets merged into Suddha Ga, the first is Sadharana Ga and the second, Anthara Ga, which is also Vikriti. The Ma which has three Srutis less is Suddha Ma. When Pa has only three Srutis, it is called Trisruti Pa, which is also Vikriti. When Pa obtains the fourth Sruti of Sa, it is called Kaisika Pa in spite of its four Srutis. This is also a Vikriti Swaram. When Pa has four Srutis less, Dha gets one of the Srutis of Pa and thus has four Srutis, which is also a Vikriti. So also when Sa has one Sruti less, Ri gets 4 Srutis, which additional one is a Vikriti Swaram. To sum up, then, the 12 Vikriti Swarams are :—

Sa—Suddham and Achyutam—2
Ni—Kaisikam and Kakali—2
Dha—while obtainining one of the Srutis of Pa—1
Ri—when obtaining one of Sa—1
Pa—Tirusruti Pa and Kaisika Pa—2
Ma—Suddham and Achyutam—2
Ga—Kaisikam and Kakali—2

The Suddha Swarams are 7. The three Swarams are, Ri in Sa, Ma in Ga and Dha in Pa.

The method adopted by Sarnga Dev for determining Swarams could be clearly understood by those who know the working and harmony of nature. There could be nothing there which they cannot understand. This is the place where the high water mark of South Indian music is clearly seen. Just as it is clearly stated that the Sthayis should proceed at the ratio of 1, 2, 4 &c., so also the Swarams of a Sthayi, should proceed with a uniform interval. We shall see how Sarnga Dev proceeds. He says, first take a Veena with 22 strings. Tune the first string so that it may produce the lowest possible sound. The next string must be tuned to sound the next possible note. There must be no possible sound between the two strings. So when the 22 strings are tuned on the above principle, the Srutis ascend in a regular serial order till the octave is reached. This is a naturai series, and this has been stated in the easiest language possible In addition to this he gives the measurement of each Sruti also in the clearest language. But there is also something occult attacned to it. He did not dilate upon it, because he knew that men of learning will easily read between the lines.

When a stone is thrown in the middle of placid water, waves are formed round the central point which gradually increase in diameter and decrease in intensity at a regular uniform interval. The vibrations of a Swaram are of the same nature. The Swarams in a wire proceed upwards at regular uniform intervals, whereas the Sthanams in the wire go on in an inverse ratio. This is what Sarnga Dev meant when he said that the Sthayis should proceed upward at the uniform ratio of 1, 2, 4, 8 &c. If the Swarams proceed at the ratio of 1 to 2 in the first octave, it is 2 to 4 in the second, and 4 to 8 in the third. But the length of wire for each octave is exactly the reverse. If the first octave finishes in the first half of the length of the string, the second octave finishes in the quarter of the length, the third in ⅛ of the length and the fourth octave in $\frac{1}{16}$ of the length, and so on. The vibrations and length of wire vary in inverse ratio. Just as the first wave in the pond has a large intensity and small diameter, and just as the diameter increases, the intensity diminishes, so is the case with sound waves also. Again, when a ray of light from the eye proceeds in a triangular form and falls upon an object, at the apex of the triangle the sight is distinct while it gets obscure at the base. But at the apex the area seen is small, but at the base the area seen is extensive so as to include even two hills. So is the case with sound waves also. Scholars will acknowledge that this rule is true of all objects of nature. The growth of leaves, flowers, petals of flowers, and seeds of grass, herbs and plants, the inner growth of trees, the growth of animals, the growth of pearls, corals, and oysters, and the inner growth of the layers of the earth—all these show a regular uniformity in their upward and onward progress just like sound waves. In the same way, heaven and earth and all creation obey the law of regular growth, support each other in their harmonious working and thus declare the omnipotence of the Creator. We all believe in what the Holy Bible says, "In the beginning was the Word." The whole world was created by the Word and the self same Word was the life. The same Word was the cause of the variety of Nadam, which manifested itself as Sapta Swarams, as the different Srutis and later on as Geetams. If Nadam did not obey the law of uniformity, there could be no harmony of sweetness.

Sweetness is caused by uniformity. Whether they be colours, or sounds, or tastes, or qualities, or smells, or sensations of touch or knowledge, unless they be proportionately made up, they will be abhorred by every one. If in an article which is compounded of five different ingredients, there is one more or less, it will not taste well. This is our every day experience. The same with taste. So if sound, its harmony and the calculations of it in a wire vary, how could it be sweet? It will be just the reverse. The series of sounds which have no uniform ratio between them will only form an abhorrent discord. Will musicians of repute accept such strange sounds and measurements? Every one must agree that any system, which has no uniformity in length of wire and its corresponding sounds, must be wrong. The very fact that it is said that the octaves must proceed upwards in the ratio of one to two, and that the series must proceed gradually with a uniform interval between them without admitting other possible sounds between, shows that the ancients had clearly understood the uniformity of the law of nature. People are quite at liberty to form their own theories with their own measu ements and put them into practical use also. But, what we object to is, that they should call it the system of Sarnga Dev.

In spite of the clear statement that the series must be uniformly progressive without admitting other Swarams between, one writer says that the octave should be divided into 22 equal parts.

Another locates Ma in the exact middle of the whole string and distributes 9 Srutis equally in the half length, namely 3 Ris, 2 Gas and 4 Mas. The other half he eqally divides into 13 parts, 4 for Pas, 3 for Dhas, 2 for Nis and 4 for Sas.

Yet another mentions 4 Ris as well as 4 Dhas. This class of writers at least made equal divisions of the strings. But knowing that the length of wire will not exactly correspond with the sounds produced, they left off saying anything about the other half of the string.

Yet others, though they say the sounds must be of equal inlervals, they forget the fact altogether; give measurements which do not agree either in sounds or the length of the string, and try to multiply them with fractions for equalising them, which has landed them in difficulties. Those irregularities have been dealt with altogether. Their chief errors will also be pointed out hereafter from time to time.

How strange it is that the opinions of the ancient musicians of this Bharatakhandam noted for its excellence, and which was the birth place of so many eminent sages should be thus set aside and disregarded! How strange it is that their Sootrams should be changed and mutilated and mis-interpreted and added to, in this reckless manner!! The ancients, who were strong on account of the excellence of their penance and who were clever in Yogam, Gnanam, Vatham, Medicine, Astrology, Oviam, Geetam, use of weapons, Mantram, Vasyam and Occultism, have reserved the keynote of each science for the purpose of teaching it in person to those best fitted to receive it, and so have not stated them explicitly. This fact is mentioned in the books. Some have become perplexed owing to the voluminous pages of the books. Many have discredited them as pure lies. There were only very few, who understood those mystic keynotes by learning them in person from those eminent men who knew them. They have said in their works.

"They are so hard-hearted that they will not tell them to every one they see."

"They will not tell the truth to anyone. Those who tell others are ignorant and wicked."

II.

"Try to understand the mystery which is buried without your knowledge, and prosper."

"Those who were willing to help, wrote work, but hid the mystic truth from others."

"The science that is not learnt with the help of the Guru cannot be acquired even by the sweat of the body."

"It (the mystery) will seem to be plain to the eye of everyone, but, without the favour of the Guru, it can never be acquired."

The mystery of each science is taught at their last moments to a worthy disciple of theirs whom they could trust. In the Chakram with fortythree triangles which is established in all the temples by Sankarachar
iar, the Jagat Guru, all is plain with the exception of one little secret, which is the key of the whole Chakram, and which is not visible to the ordinary individual. Without knowing the secret key the chakram could never be understood. The key is so arranged that while you say thirteen it really means, fourteen. that by an easy sign or writing on the ground you must indicate one should be added. In the same way there are such hidden mysteries in other sciences which cannot be understood unless told by the Guru. The same applies to the science of music. This secret has been revealed from time to time only to a select few and put into practice either by the special favour of God or as a result of unremitting labour. Such secrets pertaining to the science of music and the system of their interpretation will be mentioned later on.

The Calculation of a Sthayi.

What we have to notice specially now is, to determine the measurements of Swarams from the fact that the Madhya Sthayi finishes in the first half of the string and the vibrations of the Swarams from the fact that the Sthayis proceed in Geometrical Progression. Let us assume for this purpose that the length of wire is 32 inches, and the vibrations of Sa 540. The reason for the above assumption will be mentioned under the heading "The Srutis of South Indian music." The measurements of all writers have been reduced to this uniform standard, so that they may be easily compared. Lovers of Indian music! We have determind to write at length and bring this affair to a satisfactory conclusion so that others may not laugh at us for quarrelling without understanding each other. But it is not an easy matter to reduce the various measurements to this particular standard. However, we have brought everything to a uniform standard and have given it in the form of Tables which might be easily understood by all.

We know very well that the ancients skilled for ages in the Science of Astronomy, have devised mnemonics (Dhruva Vakkiams) for remembering the minute calculations. The primary numbers are called Moola Dhruvams, and the resultant integers are called Varundhravams (products). Thus they have made this science easy as is seen from their writings here and there. From all this, it is clearly seen that our ancestors must have had an easy key for even the most difficult of calculations. As we have no such keys in vogue at the present day, we have made use of the Table of Logarithms of an eminent English Mathematician noted for his learning and researches.

TABLE 44.

Showing the 22 Srutis of Indian music according to Sarnga Dev, the author of Sangeeta Ratnakaram.

No. of the Swaram or the Sruti.	Name of the Swaram or Sruti.	Logarithm.	No. of the Logarithm.	No. of vibrations of Swarams if SA=540.	Decimal fractions showing the places of Swarams if the Adhara SA=1.	The Location of Swarams in a wire 32 inches long.	The interval between Srutis.	Cents.	Cents for the interval between Swarams.
1	2	3	4	5	6	7	8	9	10
0	S_1	0	1·000000	540	1·0000000	32·000000		0	
1	S_2	·01368318	1·032008	557·28432	0·9689844	31·007501	·9925	54·55	54·54½
2	S_3	·02736636	1·065041	575·12268	0·9389310	30·045792	·9617	109·09	54·54½
3	S_4	·04104955	1·099131	593·53128	0·9098095	29·113904	·9319	163·64	54·54½
4	R_1	·05473273	1·134313	612·52848	0·8815912	28·210918	·9030	218·18	54·54½
5	R_2	·06841591	1·17062	632·1348	0·8542482	27·335942	·8750	272·73	54·54½
6	R_3	·08209909	1·208086	652·3686	0·8277522	26·488102	·8478	327·27	54·54½
7	G_1	·09578227	1·246758	673·2493	0·8020800	25·666560	·8215	381·82	54·54½
8	G_2	·10946545	1·286665	694·8000	0·7772029	24·870493	·7916	436·36	54·54½
9	M_1	·12314864	1·327849	717·0379	0·7530978	24·099130	·7714	490·91	54·54½
10	M_2	·13683182	1·370351	739·989	0·7297400	23·351680	·7474	545·45	54·54½
11	M_3	·15051500	1·414214	763·67556	0·7071068	22·627418	·7243	600	54·54½
12	M_4	·16419818	1·45948	788·1192	0·6851755	21·925616	·7018	654·55	54·54½
13	P_1	·17788136	1·506196	813·34584	0·6639245	21·245584	·6800	709·09	54·54½
14	P_2	·19156455	1·554406	839·37924	0·6433325	20·586640	·6589	763·64	54·54½
15	P_3	·20524773	1·604160	866·2464	0·6233790	19·948128	·6385	818·18	54·54½
16	P_4	·21893091	1·655507	893·9732	0·6040447	19·329430	·6187	872·73	54·54½
17	D_1	·23261409	1·708457	922·5878	0·5853100	18·729920	·5995	927·27	54·54½
18	D_2	·24629727	1·763182	952·1183	0·5671563	18·149000	·5809	981·82	54·54½
19	D_3	·25998045	1·819619	982·5948	0·5495656	17·586099	·5629	1036·36	54·54½
20	N_1	·27366364	1·877862	1014·04548	0·5325206	17·040659	·5454	1090·91	54·54½
21	N_2	·28734682	1·937968	1046·50272	0·5160040	16·512128	·5285	1145·45	54·54½
22	S	·30103000	2·000000	1080·00000	0·5000000	16·000000	·5121	1200	54·54½

The calculations of the Dwavimsati Srutis.

We shall first see how the 22 Srutis are a gradually ascending series beginning from Adhara SA and ending with Tara SA which is its double, according to the theory of Sarnga Dev.

The Logarithm of 1 is 0 and that of 2 is ·3010300. Now let us see how the 22 Srutis proceed gradually from 0 to ·3010300 without admitting any interval between. We can obtain the Logarithms for the Sthanams from 1 to 22 if we divide the Logarithm of 2 by 22 and multiply the quotient by the numbers of the Srutisthanams one after another by 1, 2, 3, 4 &c. Now, if we divide the Logarithm of 2 or ·3010300 by 22 we get ·01368318 or the Logarithm of the first Sthanam. This is the Logarithm of the second of the four Srutis of Adhara SA. Multiplying this by 2 we get ·02736636. This is the Logarithm of the third of the Srutis of Adhara SA. Again if we multiply the Logarithm of the first Sruti by 3 we obtain ·04104955, which is the Logarithm of the fourth SA. Likewise we may arrive at the Logarithms of the 22 Sthanams. They stand in the ratio of $2^{\frac{1}{22}}$, $2^{\frac{2}{22}}$; $2^{\frac{3}{22}}$, and so on and nothing more. The Logarithms for the 22 Sthanams may be found in column 3 of Table 44. If we determine the numbers for the Logarithm between 1 and 22, we may notice how they gradually rise in an equal ratio between Adhara SA=1 and Tara SA=2. We have stated before, that the Logarithm of 1 is 0. Therefore for Logarithm 0 the number is 1. This is Adhara SA. So the Logarithm of the Adhara SA is 0. For Logarithm of the first Sruti or ·01368318 the number is 1·032008. The Logarithm of the second Sruti or ·02736636 obtains the number 1·065041. The same process will give the numbers for the series which may be found in column 4 of the Table. Here we may see clearly how the series proceed gradually with equal intervals. To test the correctness of these figures we have given their decimal fractions also correct to six; seven and even eight places. If we take the decimals only to two or three places they will be found still more easy to demonstrate. However, we shall do well to compare at least four places of decimals, so that the calculations may not in course of time get out of reckoning gradually as was the case with the Srutis. Just as we found that the Logarithm of 2 was ·3010300, so we shall see clearly that the Logarithm ·3010300 gets 2 as its number.

The calculation of vibrations for the 22 Srutis.

We know that the theory of Sarnga Dev is—that if the first Sthayi is 1, its Octave must be 2. If Adhara SA is 1, its Octave must be 2. We noticed beforehand the 22 intervals between 1 and 2. In the same way we must observe how the number of vibrations beginning from Adhara SA=540, proceed upwards in equal ratio for the 22 Sthanams. Adhara SA has 540 vibrations per second. This has been noted in column 5 of the Table as 1×540=540 or the first number. In the same way, if we multiply the number 1·032008 (equal to the Logarithm of the first Sruti found in col. 4) by 540 we get 557·28432. Likewise, the number 1·065041 equal to the Logarithm of the second Sruti when multiplied by 540 gives 575·12268. So also, the numbers of the Logarithms for the 22 Srutis when multiplied by 540 respectively, will give us the number of vibrations found in column 5 of the Table. The 22nd Srutisthanam will end with 2 × 540 or 1080 vibrations.

Till now we have noticed at what lengths the 22 Srutis occur in the wire and the number of vibrations of each Sruti. It is better to keep the calculations of the Srutisthanams in decimals and ensure their correctness up to two, three or four places. But if we take the calculations by vulgar fractions, the process of multiplying will cause much difference.

The calculation showing where the 22 Srutis occur in a wire 32 inches long.

We must next proceed to locate the 22 Srutisthanams in a wire 32 inches long. The Adhara SA occurs at the commencement and the Tara SA in the exact middle of the whole length of a wire. Therefore we must find out how the 22 Srutis gradually decrease in the length of the wire within half the total length. The Adhara SA has 540 vibrations. ∴ sounds at the Meru which is 1. We have shown in the fifth column of Table 44, how the first Sruti has 557·28432 vibrations. If we divide 540 by 557·28432 we get ·9689844. In the same manner if 540 be divided by 575·12268, which is the number of vibrations of the second Sruti, we get ·9389310. In the same manner, if we proceed to divide 540 by the number of vibrations of the third, the fourth and the fifth etc., Srutis, we will obtain the lengths of the wire given in column 6.

We get ½ or ·5 for the 1080 vibrations opposite the 22nd Sruti. This shows how the 22 Srutis gradually decrease in the length of the wire from Adhara SA which is 1 to Tara SA which is ½ without admitting any other possible Sruti in the interval.

We shall next proceed to note where the Srutis occur in the wire which is 32 inches long. We all know that the Adhara SA sounds in the Meru, and the Tara SA sounds at the 16th inch or one half. These 22 Srutis must occur within these 16 inches, and they must rise step by step from the Adhara SA. Not only they should rise step by step but must not admit of any other Sruti in the interval and the Sthayi must come to an end exactly at half the length of the wire. In the sixth column of the above Table, may be found the different lengths of the wire for the 22 Srutis in half the total length. We shall now proceed to locate them.

If we take the Meru to be 1, the 32 inches end there. So it becomes 1 × 32 or 32. This is the first measurement in column 7 of the Table. The first Sruti or the second of the four Srutis of SA, is ·9689844 of the total length (see the second number in col. 6). If we multiply this by 32 we get 31·007501 which is the second measurement in col. 7. Likewise, if the 2nd, 3rd, 4th, 5th and the 6th Srutisthanams in col. 6 be multiplied by 32 we shall be able to get the particular length in which each Swaram should sound. ·5 of the 22nd Sthanam when multiplied by 32 gives us 16. All these measurements are found in col. 7. We may notice a particular uniformity and harmony between the Swarams if we look into these calculations.

The harmony between the Srutis.

Just as the numbers in col. 1 are of a uniform order, just as they increase by a common uniform ratio, in the same way the figures in the other columns also have a certain uniformity in them. Any Sthanam may be taken as the standard and the measurements proceeded with, there will be no difference in the ratio. 1 will be to 4 as 4 is to 7; 7 will be to 10 as 4 is to 7; 5 will be to 9 as 1 is to 5 or 9 is to 13 or 13 is to 17 or 17 to 21. 9 will be to 17 and 13 to 21 just as 1 is to 9. 13 will be to the 3rd number of Tara Sthayi or 25 just as 1 is to 13 or 9 to 21. All measurements in the other columns will have the same uniformity.

We might also go a little deeper and see a little more clearly how these Sruti Sthanams stand in equal proportion to one another without any difference. The number obtained for the Logarithm of the first Sruti in col. 4 when multiplied by itself gives us the figure for the second Srutisthanam. In the same way, if the second be multiplied by the number of the first we obtain that of the third.
For example,

1·032008 × 1·032008 = 1·065041. If this be again multiplied by 1·032008 it gives us 1.099131, the figure for the third Sruti. If this again be multiplied by 1·032008 we get 1·134313, the figure for the fourth Sruti. In the same manner every figure when multiplied by that of the first Srutisthanam gives that of its next Srutisthanam. Again, the figure for the first Sruti in col. 6 namely ·9689844 when multiplied by itself gives the figure for the Second Sruti and which multiplied by that of the first Sruti gives the figure for the third, Etc.
For example,

·9689844 × ·9689844 = ·9389310; and ·9389310 × ·9689844 = ·9098095. In the same manner the figure for each Sruti when multiplied with that of the first, will give us the figure for the next. Likewise, if the figure for the fourth Sruti found in cols. 4 and 6 be multiplied by itself we get the figure for the 8th Sthanam which is its *vargam*, and if the same figure be multiplied by itself thrice, we get the figure for the 12th Sthanam which is its *ghanam*, and the same when multiplied four times by itself gives the figure for the 16th Sthanam which is its *varga vargam*. In the same manner, any figure taken, when dealt with according to the above rule, will give us proportinate results.

We might also notice another uniformity. The figure for the first Sruti in col. 4 if multiplied by the figure for the same in col. 6 will give us 1. (1·032008 × ·9689844 = 1). The same holds good if the figures for the second Sruti be so multiplied (1·06504 × ·9389310 = 1). The figures for the 22nd Sruti when multiplied together give us the same result. (2 × ·5 = 1). Men of knowledge will clearly understand these truths.

Again, if we look at the cents calculation in cols. 9 and 10, we may find that they proceed by a common ratio, 54·54 or nearly 54½.

Besides this, the decimal fractions in col. 6 when multiplied in a particular order will always give us the product ½. For example, multiply the figures for Adhara and Tara Sa, or those for the first and the 21st Srutis, or those for the second and the 20th Srutis, or those for the 3rd and the 19th; the result will always be ½. In the same way, if the figures for Adhara and Tara Sa in col. 4 and for the 1st and 21st, 2nd and the 20th, 3rd and the 19th be multiplied together the product will always be 2. The middle or the 11th Sruti must be muliplied by itself to obtain the same result.

These calculations might be multiplied and explained in many different ways. But what we have said is quite enough to determine the exact position of the Srutisthanams.

This is the method given by Sarnga Dev for determining Srutis. We firmly assert that no other method could give the proper measurements, if, according to Sarnga Dev, the two Sthayis must be in the proportion of 1 to 2, and the 22 wires should produce a gradually ascending series of 22 Srutis in the octave without admitting any other sound in the middle. Men of understanding must certainly admit this. Unless the rungs of a ladder are equidistant, it will be impossible to go up and down the ladder. This is our everyday experience. If there is no such uniformity in the ladder of sounds it will be a stumbling block. It is strange that they have not understood this. They are not to be blamed. They stumbled because they tried to multiply the fractions head downwards. The Srutis also shared the same fate and became a discordant series. Each one believed that he was following the method of Sarnga Dev and it would be inexplicable to others, with the result they all completely strayed away from the method of Sarnga Dev. These writers who said they had all followed the one method, differed very much from each other. And they tried to perpetuate their different methods and tried to reconcile them with those of modern music by obtaining supporters for their respective theories; yea, they went a step further and invented instruments to support the fraud. They only excite our pity. We fear that the South Indian music will share the fate of the ship that is caught in the middle of the ocean during a terrific storm and darkness caused by the eclipse of the Sun in the sign of Thulam (துலாம்.)

Applying the principle of changing the Gramam to their new Swarams which stray away altogether from the principle of Sarnga Dev and finding they are not at all in agreement with his calculation, some of them say that a few Srutis are newly formed in the process. One of them says that three new Srutis generate from the Shadja Gramam, Madhyma Gramam and Gandhara Gramams respectively, while another foreseeing danger such a process and knowing the Srutis will not agree, quietly omits them. Yet another hoping that if there were 53 Srutis in the octave the trouble might be got rid of, establishes 53 Sthanams by the Sa-Pa series and says he has picked out 22 out of them. Are not the theories which try to establish 23, 24, 25 and even 53 Srutis in the octave quite contrary to Sarnga Dev and his 22 Srutis? We should particularly note that the 22 Srutis, when subject to change of Gramam, should not vary in their respective calculations or sounds and that they should satisfy the principle of harmony of Vadi and Samvadi. If the 22 Srutis are of a uniform order in calculations as well as sounds they would certainly stand the test of Vadi and Samvadi in any Gramam, beginning from any Srutis whatever. If two ladders whose rungs are equidistant and of the same size were tied together exactly one over the other or tied in such a way that a rung of one is on any of the rungs of the other either in the three quarters or half or quarter parts, they will certainly serve the purpose of going up and down conveniently. But if the two have different kinds of rungs which are not equidistant, the use of them separately will certainly be difficult. But if we attempt to tie ¾ of one with the ¼ of the other or ⅓ of one with the ½ of the other the results will be the production of a number of rungs at irregular intervals. The difficulties and objections raised against the system of 22 Srutis are to be traced to their irregular measurements. It will be more to the point, if the advocates of the system will reduce to notation the Geetams which they sing and bring it into practical use. On the other hand, they adopt a system which is unnecessary and impracticable, and of which they are ignorant, and carry on a war of words which will certainly not be accepted by men with knowledge. Again, the more they attempt at change of Grahaswaram, the more the absurdities accumulate and land them in difficulties just like the accumulations of dust of the iron pestle of the Yadavakulam. Even these absurdities will have to be noted here. This will help people to understand whether the Srutis according to Sarnga Dev or the Srutis according to these authors are correct.

The principle of changing Graham according to Sarnga Dev.

We noticed till now, the system of Sarnga Dev where the 22 Srutis are derived in the octave with the aid of the first Veena with 22 strings where they are arranged in a gradually ascending series without admitting any other sound in the middle. Let us now notice his principle of changing Graham. He says that the seven Swarams occurring in the 4th, 7th, 9th, 13th, 17th, 20th and the 22nd Sthanams of the first Veena should be made to sound in the 3rd, 6th, 8th, 12th, 16th, 19th and the 21st string of the second Veena. This is exactly the same as beginning the ourth Sruti of Sa from the third Sruti of Sa and proceeding upwards so that the seven original Swarams occur at the Sthanam one Sruti less. In the same manner, if the fourth Sa starts from the second Sa then each Sruti will occur in places 2 Srutis less. So Ga and Ni will occur on Ri and Dha. Thirdly, if the fourth Sa commences on the first Sa, Ri and Dha lose three places and occur on the 2nd, 3rd and the 4th Srutis of Sa and Pa. Fourthly, when the fourth Sa commences on the 22nd Sthanam, Sa occurs on Ni, Ma on Ga, and Pa on Ma.

Beloved Readers! we understand from the work of Sarnga Dev that the names given by our ancestors to the Srutis were causing confusion even during his time. After him many writers have used many Srutis and Sruti names which are entirely conflicting with one another. To make matters worse, some modern writers have invented 53 Srutis and such fancy names as Vadiga and Chodika. So we have only numbered the Srutisthanams so that you may not get confused with the different names and that one right conclusion might be arrived at as regards Srutis. We do not make a display by giving a number of names of which we are not sure. We give only as many names as are necessary for a clear elucidation.

What we have to clearly note is the fact that just as the numbers 1, 2, 3, 4 have a certain uniform ratio between them, just like the regular rungs of a ladder, so these Sthanams are also in regular uniformity with the same ratio in whatever direction they may be taken. If they do not have such a ratio, it is a matter well known to men of understanding. that they will never agree with the first Swaram, when shifted here and there. If the 4 SAS, 3 RIS. and 2 Srutis of GA were not of equal intervals how could the third Sruti of RI agree with or coincide with the third Sruti of SA, and the first GA with the fourth SA, when SA commences on the 22nd Srutisthanam? Sarnga Dev made mention of a superior method where the Swarams also agree in the same manner. It is clear that he never advocated Srutis with unequal intervals.

Those who have doubts might easily clear them if they look at the Table in the next page.

He says that when we take a Sruti less in each case beginning from SA 4 we get the Moorchanas of the Sapta Swarams. This he calls Shadja Gramam. What we have to note here is, that if SA should commence from the 22nd Sruti of NI it is absolutely necessary that there should be a Sthayi below. For the first Sruti should be the lowest possible one. and so any Sthanam below the first SA cannot possibly exist, for it cannot sound. So we should understand that the change of Graham is possible only from the Madhya Sthayi. We clearly see that for purposes of singing Graha Swaram and fixing the measurements there should be a Sthayi before Madhya Sthayi and one after.

Shadja Gramam.

Now we commence the Shadja Gramam. This has 22 Srutis with 4 SAS, 3 RIS, 2 GAS, 4 MAS, 4 PAS, 3 DHAS, and 2 NIS. Wherever we might commence the I Sruti, the Sapta Swarams should be similar in the measurement of the Sruti.

Madhyma Gramam.

In the same manner, this Gramam has 22 Srutis with 4 SAS, 3 RIS, 2 GAS, 4 MAS, 3 PAS, 4 DAS and 2 NIS, while the Sapta Swarams should be used in the order of their Srutis in the various Ganams We also note that PA has one Sruti less or in other words, the third Sruti of PA is used as its PA and the fourth PA goes along with DHA. While all the other Srutis sound in their own Sthanam, PA alone sounds in its 3rd Sruti instead of the fourth. All the other Swarams remain Suddha Swarams.

Gandhara Gramam.

Next comes Gandhara Gramam the one that became celestial. He says that this Gramam should also have 22 Srutis with 4 SAS (1. 2. 3, &4); 2 RIS (5 and 6). 4 GAS (7, 8, 9 and 10). 3 MAS (11, 12 and 13), 3 PAS (14. 15 and 16). 3 DHAS (17, 18 and 19) and 3 NIS (20, 21 and 22). When they change the Graham they must occur with the same regular intervals. Here, all the other Swarams with the exception of SA, MA and NI lose the character of Suddha Swarams. For, the RI instead of being the 7th Sruti becomes the 6th, the GA becomes the 10th instead of the 9th Sruti. PA becomes the 16th instead of the 17th Sruti, and DHA becomes the 19th Sruti instead of the 20th. Here RI, PA and DHA have each one Sthanam less, while GA has one Sthanam more. So four Swarams get shifted from their usual Sthanam thus making Ganam difficult and involved. Perhaps on account of this difficulty all the great Vidwans had it banished to the celestial regions. We do not know what other things will share the same fate. We pray that God may save at least the remnants of South Indian music from sharing the same fate.

III.

TABLE 45.

The following Tables show clearly some of the remarks made about changing Grahams.

Shadja Gramam.

According to Sangeetha Ratnakaram.

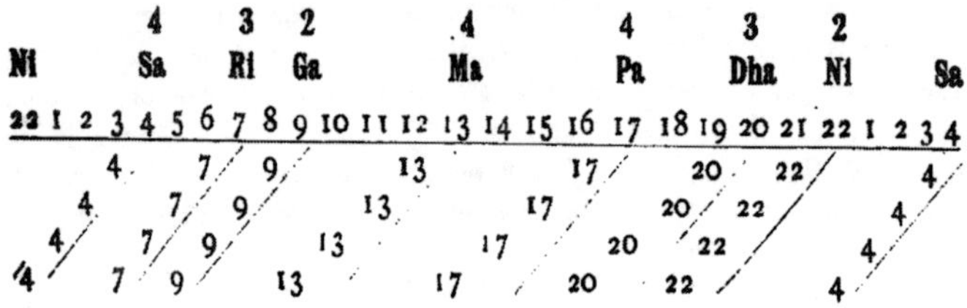

Madhyma Gramam.

According to Sangeetha Ratnakaram.

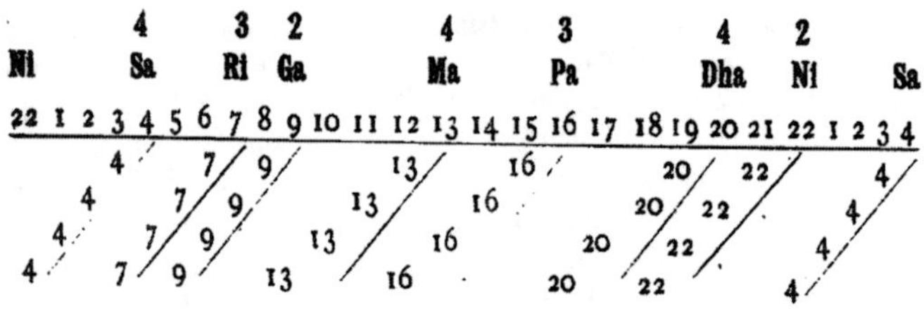

Gandhara Gramam.

According to Sangeetha Ratnakaram.

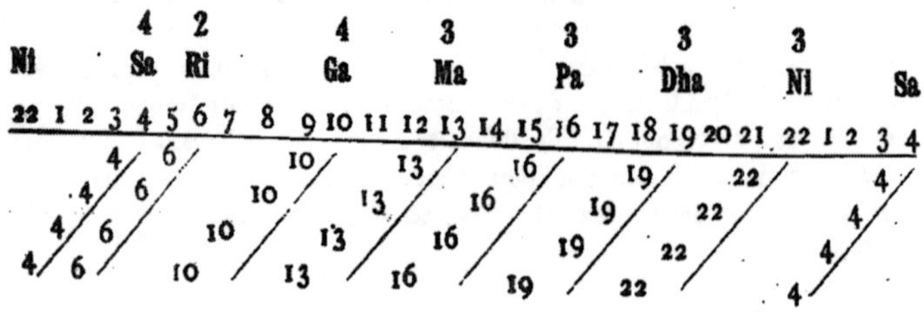

As Sarnga Dev mentions that it was so banished even before his time, it is clear that it went out of use ages ago. We are afraid that the same might be the fate of the Shadjama and Madhyma Gramams belonging to this GA.

In the Table, the opinion of Sarnga Dev who said that they should have the same harmony while they changed the Graham, is indicated by numbers. For, the measurements given by Sarnga Dev for the 22 Srutis have the uniform intervals as in the numbers 1, 2, 3, 4 &c., and those measurements and sounds exactly correspond with these. I have clearly proved there that they would not admit of any other measurement. I need not therefore repeat it here. The measurements found in the Table, when compared with the numbers found in the Table of Gramams, will be found to be exactly the same. They do not differ even in the slightest degree and they do not admit of any unequal intervals in the middle. While matters stand thus, one author boasts that he has discovered 2 more Srutis over 22, (22+2=24), another 3 more Srutis (22+3=25) while yet another claims to have discovered 31 more (or 31+22=53). Men of understanding will never accept these.

The application of Sa-Pa and Sa-Ma measurements to the theory of the 22 Srutis of Sarnga Dev.

We know that Sarnga Dev has freely used the SA-PA and SA-MA systems which stand in the relation of Vadi and Samvadi. He says that where 8 Srutis occur between two Swarams they stand in the relation of SA-MA. and where 12 Swarams occur between two they stand in the relation of SA-PA. In other words, the 9 Srutis omitting the 1 will form SA-MA series, and the 13 Srutis omitting the 1, the SA-PA series. All Swarams must conform to this system. This implies that if the Srutis were of unequal intervals and measurements they will never agree.

It is to be noted that every one, who advocates any system of Srutis says that he has proceeded by the SA-PA and SA-MA series. But their Swarasthanams are not of a uniform interval. Though this is contrary to the system of Sarnga Dev they will swear it is his. We have proved clearly by the Tables 15 and 16 on pages (306-307) that the 22 Srutis obtain perfection in Tara SA, the SA-PA series in the 13th Sthayi and the SA-MA series in the 9th. The same is repeated in the 9th column of Table 44 which gives the system of Srutis of Sarnga Dev on page 406. When we proceed by nines we get the SA-MA series. If we multiply the cents against number 9 by 2 (*i.e.,*) if 490·91 be multiplied by two, we get the cents for the 18th place which is the next one, and then the cents for the fifth Sthanam. So when the cents of the Srutisthanams are multiplied by the numbers 4, 5 and 6 in order, we get those for the 22 Srutis.

In the same manner, if the cents against the 13th Sruti 709·09 be multiplied by 2, 3, 4 and 5 we get the cents for the 22 Srutis of the octave. These intervals are completely perfect without even the slightest difference of a fraction. In this Table if MA and PA are reckoned from the fourth SA, they will appear as the 12th and the 16th Sthanams respectively.

We shall presently see that if we do not admit of more than 22 Srutis in the octave according to Sarnga Dev and others, there will be a slight trouble when the change of Graham is made. In order to understand this clearly, let us compare the conflicting opinions of all advocates of the Dwavimsati Srutis.

A comparison of the different opinions of writers as regards the Srutis in use in Indian Music.

We see clearly that among the writers about Sruti. Sarnga Dev is the primary author and that he has followed the method of Bharata who lived long before him. Writers in India and in the Western countries profess to follow the system of Sarnga Dev but in reality they make us of the measurements $\frac{2}{3}$ and $\frac{3}{4}$. But this is not at all the system of Sarnga Dev. They are ready to raise objections when we say that their method is contrary to that of Sarnga Dev. So it is absolutely necessary we should compare his with those of others in measurement, fractions and cents.

TABLE 46.

Here, in this Table, I have marked the measurements of Srutis of different writers in a Veena String which is exactly 16 inches long, which is the first half of a Veena wire 32 inches in length. Their measurements are accurately marked in the Madhya Sthayi 16 inches long. Those who want to test the accuracy of their measurements by sounding them in the Veena might easily mark their Swarasthanams by fixing a long strip of paper 16 inches long against the column opposite their names. They may then fix the frets in their Veenas from the Meru up to 16 inches and verify the Swarasthanams on the Veenas. The bridge of the frets should not be broad but very thin so that they may indicate exact measurements. They must be so made as to be fixed and removed with the gretest ease. The Merusthanam should not be high. for then the strings will have to be held tight which might dislocate the Swsrasthanams. The difference in frets between the Meru and the other Swarasthanams should be the thickness of a piece of paper and no more. But it must be understood that this is not for the purpose of producing music on the Veena but only for testing the Swarasthanams.

TABLE 47.

This Table marks the Swarasthanam in a wire 32 inches long. This is for the purpose of testing the accuracy of the measurements given before.

TABLE 48.

This Table shows the fractions corresponding to the measurements of Swarasthanams in the wire.

TABLE 49.

This Table gives the cents calculations of the different Sthanams bringing out the difference in the fractions. This will be useful for comparing the different views.

We shall only notice one or two important points here. The measurements of Sarnga Dev found in the first column closely follow his book. Those measurements and their uniformity should be clearly appreciated. The intervals, beginning from Adhara SA proceed upwards on a uniform ratio. In the same manner, the sound also increases gradually and finishes with 22 Srutis. We see that his superior system throws that of the others completely into the shade. Those who professed to follow his regular method followed really the method $\frac{9}{8}$ and $\frac{4}{3}$. So the systems of other writers never tally with his. There is a difference of 7 cents between the MA of Sarnga Dev (491 cents) and that of others (498) necessarily. There is also the difference of 7 cents between the PA of Sarnga Dev (709 cents) and that of others (702 cents), If the standard Swarams MA and PA are thus different, what can we expect about others? Measurements by two roads which are different will cause difference and trouble. The Table clearly shows this. Again, to bring out the discrepancy in measurements still more glaringly, if a red line be drawn from RI, in column 1 of Table 46, to all the RI Sthanams of the different writers, the line would never be a straight one! The same will be found as regards GA, DHA and NI and other Swarams. They are not of uniform intervals, nor do they follow Sarnga Dev, nor will they in any way suit Karnatic music.

Some of the Tables of other writers and their opinions have not been added here as they reached us after this Table was prepared.

Two important points which might help us arriving at the Srutis of Karnatic Music.

(Karunamirtha Sagaram in Tamil Page 512 and 513.)

Noble readers! Many eminent musicians have written about, and given their criticism on, Srutis that have been in use for the last 2400 years from the age of Pythagoras. We have seen that even today opinions vary as regards this subject. We have placed before you a few of those theories and pointed out how they contradict one another and how they are different from the systems of Sarnga Dev, Pythagoras and Ahobilar. Table 50 gives one the full idea of the subject.

From, all this it appears that if a new system, based upon all that has gone before, could be evolved which has equal and uniform measurements, then that system will certainly help us in determining the Srutis in use in South Indian music. While trying to unify the many systems that were different and arrive at the truth, I came across a few ideas which are contained in an ancient Tamil literary work. This work is considered one of the best and most ancient of Tamil works on music and one that could throw considerable light upon the controversy as regards Srutis. Moreover it has the sanction of Shastras and gives a system of Srutis which might help in reciting the Sama Vedam. With the grace of learned sages I came across these ideas which I give below.

1. I hold that the system of Srutis of Sarnga Dev is the right one for determinig the Srutis in use in Indian Music, and that no one could improve on this system.

In other words the series should proceed upwards from Athara Sa gradually with equal intervals admitting of no other Swarams in the middle.

2. Secondly, because Western Musicians as well as writers on Indian Music unanimously declare that Sa-Pa is $\frac{2}{3}$ and Sa-Ma is $\frac{3}{4}$, these two series must be approximately taken to be $\frac{2}{3}$ and $\frac{3}{4}$ respectively.

According to modern writers while proceeding by $\frac{2}{3}$ or Sa-Pa system, we finish the series a little over the octave. and while proceeding by $\frac{3}{4}$ or Sa-Ma, we finish a little below the octave. This must never be. The measurements must be so accurate that the series must end exactly with the octave neither more nor less. Then we shall arrive at the Srutis in use in South Indian music, and all doubts about Srutis will entirely vanish.

If we have the above facts in mind, we shall be able to find out how many Srutis there are in the Sthayi with their respective measurements.

Unless we adopt the system of Sarnga Dev, the Srutis cannot be changed for the purpose of Grahaswaram nor will they suit Karnatic music.

If we do not proceed by the approximate measurements of Sa-Pa and Sa-Ma the Srutis will not suit Karnatic music. Therefore we should adopt the system of Sarnga Dev along with the mysterious key for tuning instruments given by him, and the system of $\frac{2}{3}$ and $\frac{3}{4}$. By the latter we do not mean the one recommended for those who have an ear for music. but the minute and correct Sa-Pa and Sa-Ma series.

Before we arrive at the right method of determining Srutis by the above two methods, we shall do well to see what works on Isai Tamil say, which were in use among the Tamilians, the most ancient of the inhabitants of India and the most renowned in South Indian Music.

KARUNAMIRTHA SAGARAM.

EXTRACT FROM THE FIRST BOOK ON SRUTIS.

An essay on Srutis read before the All-India Music Conference held at Baroda under the kind patronage of His Highness the Gaekwar of Baroda (March 1916).

INTRODUCTION.

YOUR Highness the Gaekwar who is ever anxious to introduce reforms for the improvement of the different fine arts and handicrafts and the learned members of this august body who are assembled here with a deep interest for the advancement of Indian music! we considered hitherto the correct method of arriving at the Dwavimsati Srutis of Sarnga Dev who flourished at the beginning of the 13th century. In the same manner, I think it will clear the doubt overhanging the Srutis, if we could also consider the opinion on Srutis given by Ilankovadigal, who lived at the commencement of the 1st century, in his work Silappadikaram.

The Srutis of South Indian Music according to Isai-Tamil.

(Karunamirtha Sagaram in Tamil Page 517 — 522.)

We have noted before, that the music of the renowned ancient India was in the highest state of efficiency at one time, and that when it began to deteriorate, the scientific works of the period also were despised on the score of impracticability when compared with modern requirements.

We have also noted in the Tables given above, that though many writers have taken the greatest pains to interpret ancient musical works correctly and restore them to their original eminence, yet they have not determined the Srutis after the system of Sarnga Dev but according to their own fancy.

We were, therefore, naturally led to enquire whether South Indian music which was held to be highly efficient and scientific could have any literary support from ancient Tamil works. Though we may not fully succeed in our expectations in this respect, we are sure, at least, of certain points which are found very useful for South Indian music.

To add to this, we must understand that some of the standard Sanskrit works on music only contain those points found in South Indian music. We shall see clearly later on, how the "Chathurdandiprakasika" of Venkatamahi, the musical works of Singarachariar and the "Ragamalika" of Maha Vydianatha Iyer treat of South Indian music only. All works treating on South Indian Ragas and the 72 Melakartas contradict the ideas contained in the "Sangeeta Ratnakaram" of Sarnga Dev. We should not be led away by the fact that these works are in Sanskrit, Telugu and other languages. Just as we do not find any resemblance between the Ganam of Northern India and the "Ratnakaram" of Sarnga Dev, so also there is no resemblance between the musical works of South India written in Sanskrit, Telugu and Tamil and "Sangeeta Ratnakaram." But men of understanding will know that there is unanimity between some of the Sanskrit works of South India and the music thereof. It is but the law of nature that a child which is just able to crawl should attempt to walk, that a man who is able to walk should attempt to fly and that a man should love his wife more than the mother who gave birth to him and brought him up. Just as a man loves to describe the virtues of his mother in a foreign language though he is imperfect in it; the mysteries of South Indian music were written in a foreign language.

Those who looked upon music as a great acquisition and a lucrative one kept it as a sealed book and stood guard over it like so many *bhutams*, for fear it should be known to others. Moreover, those who wrote works on music pretended to help others but in reality they kept the key to the mysteries hidden in such a way that others might be in endless doubt.

Many thousand Keertanams of Theagaraja Iyer, who flourished at Tirvadi (Tanjore) about 60 or 70 years ago, have been destroyed by fire because those who learnt them up were unwilling to teach them to others and at the same time were indifferent about reducing them to Swara notation. When they are advised to reduce at least the remnants to notation they decline because they are afraid to commit themselves. From this, there is reason to conclude that many ancient works gradually became defunct because they kept them as sealed book without imparting the knowledge in them to others.

We have noted before that the first Sangam which patronised the three Angams of Tamil (Iyal, Isai and Natakam) for 4000 years at the time of the first Ooli (*i.e.* about 8000 years from now) along with its kings, scholars and musical works were destroyed by the sea. After their destruction even the small remnants of deteriorated musical works were brought to nought by the Buddhists and the Jains. Even those works, which remained after this, came to an end because they could not be put into practical use as there was no one to interpret the mysteries contained therein and they disappeared like the host of Ravana before thd bombs of Rama, having been eaten away by the little insect Ramabhanam. Only a few points noted down by practical musicians here and there survive so as to render traditional music possible and practicable.

It is a matter for deep regret that we are not in a position to understand Indian music as it was from the earliest times. However some of the *amsams* of it come to light through a few lines of "Silappadikaram" written by Ilankovadigal, the brother of Senguttuvan who ruled over the Tamil Chera country in ancient times *i.e.*, about 1800 years ago, by the commentary on them by Adyarkunallar and by the work of Jayankondan the Kavi Chakravarti, who wrote an annotation on the same. We read a few lines there about the singing, dancing and skill in Yal of Mathavi, and the musical genius (in playing the Yal) of the hero Kovala.

If we compare all these facts, we are led to believe that music was in a high state of efficiency at that age and must have been in a far eminent state many thousand years before that time. It goes without saying, that the three Angams of the language, namely, Iyal, Isai and Natakam, flourished when the Sangam existed at South Madura, that many of those are not in use at present and that the cause of it was their destruction by the sea. However, we are able to lay our hands on some of them, namely, the names of the works, the instruments and their description and the number of Ragas in use through the words of the author, its commentator as well as the annotator mentioned above.

The very fact that the scholars of the first Ooli and the sovereigns considered their language the first part, music the second part, and Natakam, the third, naming them Iyal-Tamil, Isai-Tamil and Nataka-Tamil respectively and improved them by devising rules of grammar for the same, proves that music was held to be very high at that time. If we notice the prosody, which is one of the sub-divisions of Iyal-Tamil, we find that all the parts thereof viz., letters, syllables, Seer, Thalai, Adi, Thodai, Koon, Ethugai and Monai are so arranged as to satisfy the rules of Music. The Ragam and Thalam are so arranged that sweet Swarams may not sound out of their Sthanams, so that the Thalam as well as the coherence of the subject may not be lost. The result of this has been the production of the different kinds of *Pah* such as Venpah, Asiriappah, Kalippah and Vanjippah and its varieties Thalisai, Thurai and Viruttham.

We may clearly understand that such productions based upon prosody and music are easily capable of being learnt by heart, are easily explainable to others and they are easily protected from the admixture of foreign element. The *pahs* which are the chief parts of Iyal-Tamil become *Puns* when sung to Music or Isai-Tamil. Though the term *pun* is a common name for Ragam and Swaram, it means *Pahs* sung to music. The *Puns* and the *Vachanams*, when used with their respective Abinayam (gestures), became Nataka-Tamil. We know that attempt at poetry can be made only when we are proficient in reading and writing.

It was only after *Pahs* were made that Isai-Tamil or music, which helped in reciting them, came into existence. After the advent of *Vachanams, Pahs* and *Puns, Abinayam* or gestures which brought out their meaning, came. Abinayam, because of its dancing and gestures, became *Natakam.* These three *amsams* of the language are as necessary for a man as his Sthoola, Sookshama and Karana Sareerams· Having this in view, our ancestors mede the three *amsams* of the language into one and called it *Muttamil.* They have devised rules of grammar also unifying the three into one. Ahatyam is considered to be its Muthal Nool. There are also others who dealt with each of them separately and wrote grammars for them whose works appear to be very comprehensive and striking. But after their destruction by the sea, smaller works which gave their purport in a condensed form, came into existence. We do not find in any language any grammar that deals with the language, *Pahs. Puns* and *Natakam* in such an exhaustive manner. From this we conclude that a literary work which dealt with Isai-Tamil or Sangeetam, and with Nataka-Tamil or Bharatam could never have been written for the first time in any other language. These two literary productions had attained high efficiency in the Tamil language from ancient times; hence the traditional name *Muttamil* for the three *amsams.* This name was not given to it yesterday or the day before. It seems to have been in use during the time of Ahastya, the author of 'Ahathiyam' and even before his time. Nor do we find the combination of these three words in any other language.

From these ancient works it is clear that although our ancestors were wanting in the requirement of modern civilisation such as steam engines, telegraphs, aeroplanes improved manners and customs, foods, drinks, I.O.U's, documents. Registration offices, courts of law, rules of procedure, time bar, and the recognition of pauperism, yet they were scholars in the Tamil language, worshipping God by their *Puns* and singing and dancing before Him, and that their sovereigns were noted for their mercy, justice, truthfulness, patience, humility, love and other virtues.

They showed themselves the very embodiment of truthfulness being bound by their words, in the midst of many trials and troubles. A promissory note written in four lines on a palmyra leaf four inches long bound them much surer than any registered document of the present day, for a period of seven succeeding generations. They made large transactions with no more living witness than fire which is easily put out after the fuel is burnt. Documents for gifts and sales were made only with the sprinkling of a handful of water which is easily sucked by the dry ground.

These three Angams of Tamil which were so helpful to one who aimed at attaining Mukti were also sources of abuse. When music which was helpful for the salvation of the soul was used for inferior purposes, it was but natural that it should degenerate into a means of livelihood. Those who used it for such mean purposes would never care for its higher uses. When it lost prestige to such an extent, it naturally followed that it was seldem made use of and gradually stifled altogether. We know how the gold lace of the turban rests on the head and how the same in the shoe rests on the foot. Such has been the state of music patronised by crowned heads in ancient times and by the poor at the modern day.

We see the eminence of music as one of the finest of arts when we enquire into it. That the civilisation of a country and its inhabitants is proportionate to their attainments in music is accepted by learned men. When we apply this test to the

Tamilians, we find that they were very highly civilised at a very early stage of their existence. It is said that the ancient inhabitants of South Madura were using 12,000 Ragas with 14, 49, 84 and even 103 Moorchanas in place of seven Moorchanas of the Seven Swarams, and were using Veenas with 17, 27, 100 and even 1000 strings. Their science of music was also proportionately of a high order.

There are some verses in Silappadikaram regarding music, which though a small part of a long story, describe to perfection an important *amsam* of music. This is a matter for gratification. Not only are those verses difficult to understand, but some of the words used there are not found in any modern work. Many precious words have gone out of use altogether. It is also difficult to understand the measurements of Ragas which were then in use. Moreover the commentators have made use of certain arguments well known in those days thinking that people who came 1000 years after them would understand them equally well. So they merely give the headings which only puzzle us. If they had been a little more explicit all the chief *amsams* of music would have been brought to light. In spite of all this, even the little that we obtain from there, are far superior to the opinions about Srutis expressed at the present day.

The grand expression "22 Srutis" is also found there. But when we go into the system of the change of Alakus of the 22 Srutis and the innumerable Moorchanas obtained while they change their Graham, the author of Sangeeta Ratnakaram is thrown into the shade. I have given below only those extracts from Silappadikaram of whose interpretation I am quite sure. The others have been omitted. However, I have examined thoroughly the system of determining the Srutis and the change of Graham. I have not made any original statements but only have made the road easy for all, so that the meaning can be clearly understood. I know I have omitted many important extracts. If scholars could see the importance of such omissions and point them out to me I am sure to include them in the second edition.

There is a slight difference between the opinions of Adyarkunallar, the commentator, and Kavichakravarti Jayankondan, the annotator, as regards a few points. The latter seems to have flourished about a hundred years before Adyarkunallar, and he deals with principles on ancient music more minutely. It is plain that Adyarkunallar based his opinions on those of Jayankondan. We have first dealt with only such matters which appear clear to us with the help of the commentaries and annotations of these two authors. Later on we have elucidated the mystic portion of their writings so that they may be clearly understood by all. One might ask why we give two interpretations, one according to what is written and one after elucidating the mysteries. We give it, so that we may not mystify our readers still more.

It will be a matter for gratification when we realise that the principles given in this work written 1800 years ago are the principles that have been in use in our Karnatic music. The same system seems to have been in vogue at the time of the author of Tholkaupiam and in the previous age. The 12 Swarams of a Sthayi and its more minute quarter tones appear to have been carried to the countries to the east of India, namely, Malaya, Siam, Anam, China, and Japan, and to the countries to the west, such as Persia, Arabia, Egypt, Asiatic Turkey and Greece. Though these countries copied it from India, so long as they were ignorant of the mystery of the Vattapalai and the right system of proceeding by the SA-PA and SA-MA series, it is no wonder that they all erred. As years rolled on, though the system of Karnatic music was lost, yet it has been preserved to a certain extent, no doubt mixed with Desikam, by means of music that has been traditionally handed down.

We may arrive at the truth by comparing music which is pure without the admixture of strange sounds and music which is so mixed. The beauty of Karnatic music is, that when its Ragas are sung without mixture according to the strict rules of Aroganam and Avaroganam they appear to be so varried and different. We have to dwell at length upon this ancient system as it will help us in eliminating the admixture of alien element and making Karnatic music pure.

The contents of Book II will be the

(i) Rules to enable all people with musical ear to sing the Karnatic Ragas pure and free from admixture.

(ii) Rules by which errors in the existing Ragas may be easily rectified.

(iii) Rules for making a Ragam with a given Aroganam and Avaroganam and for composing Gheetams, Varanams and Keertanams in the said Ragam.

We request our Tamil readers to try their best to bring to light those ancient gems of literature which are lying hidden and neglected.

Since it is our duty to know about Srutis, we shall do well to consider a few portions from the ancient Isai-Tamil, which contains informations very rare and important.

The System of Srutis and some important points as regards the Music of ancient South Tamil Country.

PRESIDENT AND MEMBERS OF THIS CONFERENCE,

All the Tamilians are aware of the fact that the Muttamil—Iyal, Isai and Natakam—was studied and was in a highly efficient state during the period of the first Sangam conducted for 4400 years in South Madura, the capital of the beautiful Tamil country. It is clear that Tamil was then divided into Iyal, Isai and Natakam and excellent rules of grammar were also devised for each of them. Isai-Tamil is now known as Music. As most of the works on Isai-Tamil treating about the Swarams and Srutis, which are the basis of all music, had become extinct or obsolete, it became impossible to know much about music. But Ilankovadigal, who flourished during the first century A. D. at the close of the third Sangam, gives a few rules on Isai-Tamil which was in use among the ancient Tamilians. It is certain that he lived before Bharata (5th centuary A. D.) and Sarnga Dev (13th centuary A. D.) We shall do well to draw our conclusions from his writings.

It appears that the ancients being cognisant of the concordant relation between the Swarams SA and PA, derived 12 Swarams in the Sthayi on this principle of SA-PA, that the 12 Palais or Rags resulted when the change of Graham was attempted in the 12 Swarams, and that seven of those Palais were considered primary. It is also clear that a Ragam with seven Swarams was sung as 14 Swarams, as it is at the present day, in the three Sthayis—hard, soft and middling. The writer has also stated that a Rasi-mandalam or cycle was divided into 12 equal parts to correspond to the 12 Swarams obtained on the principle of concordant Swarams or SA-PA (Inai) and branch Swarams or SA-MA (Kilai). that each Rasi was sub-divided into two Alakus, thus making 24, but that Ganam was made in 22 Alakus omitting an Alaku in each of the Swarams Vilari and Kaikilai (DHA and GA, E and A) and that under this principle the four kinds of Yal—Marutham, Kurinchi, Neythal and Palai—or the four leading *puns*, commenced on the Swarams SA, MA, PA and NI. He further states that each of the four kinds of Yal when commencing from SA, GA, PA and NI respectively gives rise to the four Jathis, Ahanilai, Puranilai. Arugial and Perugial. We further observe the 12,000 ancient Isais and the four Palais - Ayapalai. Vattapalai, Thirikonapalai and Chathurapalai—which have been devised so as to comprehend the Swarams, the Srutis and minute Srutis used therein. Ayapalai is defined there as the Ganam resulting from the Ragas obtained by the change of Graham of the 12 half Swarams of an octave, and Vattapalai as the Ganam resulting from the sub-division of the 12 Swarams into 24, with four Yals and four Jathis in each of those Yals, where two out of the 24 Alakus (in Vilari and Kaikilai) are left out. If we notice the ancient Ragas and Puns we come across minute Srutis such as ½ Alaku and ¼ Alaku. These are Srutis pertaining to Thirikonapalai and Chathurapalai. It is clear that the Ganam sung with half Swarams is Ayapalai, with quarter Swarams Vattapalai, with one-eighth Swarams, Thirikonapalai and that with one-sixteenth Swarams, Chathurapalai. I have given 20 Ragas in the Table as examples of Ayapalai sung with 12 half Swarams, 6 Ragas as examples of Vattapalai with quarter Swarams, 15 for Thirikonapalai with one-eighth Swarams and 11 Ragas as examples of Chathurapalai with one-sixteenth Swarams.

These Ragas have had their names changed by foreigners and are now seen under strange names

I have also given the mathematical calculations for the Swarams and the Swara Sthanams occurring in the four Palais. I have derived the Srutis so that the pitch of the Sthayis may proceed by Geometrical Progression as 1, 2, 4 and according to the system of the ancient Tamilians as well as that of Sarnga Dev where the Srutis should be a gradually ascending series with equal intervals without admitting any other possible sound between. The calculation by geometrical progression is the best method possible. By this method, I am sure, the doubt about the Dwavimsati Srutis in the octave will disappear. The term 22 Srutis was caused by the confusion arising from the system of making Ganam in 22 Alakus in Vattapalai with 24 Alakus. Ganam with 22 Srutis never existed nor could it ever exist in the future. These I affirm without the slightest doubt. When we closely observe the Isais and the minute Srutis used by the ancient Tamilians we find that, without any rigid rules, the Karnatic music has been so long in existence just as many an excellent handicraft is continued up to the present day without any definitely written rules regarding it. I may say boldly that no nation in the world speaking any language whatsoever had ever advanced in music to such an extent as to use such minute Srutis in its music. I pray to the Almightly that He would vouchsafe His grace so that every one might be enabled to appreciate and delight in the music as well as the minute Srutis used by the ancient Tamilians.

I. Determination of Srutis by Sa-Pa Series.

(Karnnamirtha Sagaram in Tamil Page 527—529.)

Silappadikaram Arangetukathai P. 90.

" ஏற்றிய குரலிளி யென்றிரு நரம்பி
னொப்பக் கேட்கு முணர்வின னாகிப்
பண்ணமை முழவின் கண்ணெறி யறிந்து
தண்ணுமை முதல்வன் றன்னொடும் பொருந்தி
வண்ணப் பட்டடை யாழ்மேல் வைத்தாங்கு "

Silappadikaram Arangetukathai P. 91.

" ஏற்றிய குரலிளி யென்றிரு நரம்பி
னொப்பக் கேட்கு முணர்வின னாகி "

என்பது பதினாற் கோவையினிடத்துக் குரனரம்பு இரட்டிக்க வரும் அரும்பாலையையும், இளிநரம்பு இரட்டிக்க வரும் மேற்செம்பாலையையும் இவைபோல அல்லாத பாலைகளையும் இசைநூல் வழக்காலே இணைநரம்பு தொடுத்துப் பாடும் அறிவினையு முடையனாயென்க."

" வண்ணப்பட்டடை யாழ்மேல் வைத்தாங் கென்பது "

பட்டடை-நரம்புகளின் இளிக்குப் பெயர்; என்னை? எல்லாப் பண்ணிற்கும் அடிமணையாதலின். வண்ணம்-நிறம். இதனையாழ் மேல்வைத் தென்க.

ஆங்கு-அசை. இளிக் கிரமத்தாலே பண்களை யாழ்மேல் வைத்தெனக் கூட்டினு மமையும்

" குரல்வா யிளிவாய்க் கேட்டனள் "

குரல்முதலாக எடுத்து இளிகுரலாக வாசித்தாளென்க,

He says in these lines that each of these Swarams must be arranged, so that it might harmonise with the other, just as Sa harmonises with Pa or Kural with Ili. We know from experience that Ili or Pa perfectly harmonises with Kural or Sa. The sweetness of the concord will be in proportion to the harmony of this Pa with Sa. He does not say here that this Pa sounds at $\frac{2}{3}$ the length of the wire. We have no reason to suppose that the ancients were unaware of this measurement. Our ancestors who were cognisant of even the minutest things in relation to music had the ability to name the order of the Sthayi and sing also on harmonious strings. So they say that one **must have such a cultivated ear so as to appreciate the complete concord of the Swarams Kural and Ili or Sa and Pa.**

It is not easy to indicate a sweet sound which could be minutely appreciated by the ear, by means of wire and calculations by the levelling rod. The internal ear as well as the nerve which differentiates auditory impressions are very subtle. The appreciation of sounds must be in proportion to the subtlety of the auditory organ. The first sound should be so appreciated and the Pa to it should be determined. Then if this Pa were made the Sa and if we proceed by the same process of fifths, we obtain the 12 Swarams. These 12 Swarams are a gradually ascending series and are as concordant with one another as Sa is to Pa. They stand in the same relation with one another as that of the husband and wife of a family with perfect concord. The Panchamam is the Mathurusthanam for all Swarams just as the Mathurusthanam, the primal cause of man, is the genitive cause of all human beings with a body. Though the male is the originative cause of all living beings, it is but a comprehensive Sookshma *amsam*. Though the first Swaram Sa comprehends in itself the Sapta Swarams, yet they obtain their shape only with the help of the Ili or the Panchamam. The relationship of Puthiran, Mithran and Chatru came by the concordant relation of Sa with Pa, and not by the individual existence of Sa like the Brahma. Therefore the seven Swarams must arrange themselves in the relation of Sa to Pa.

We must observe, why our ancestors who were such expert mathematicians who dealt with integers up to 32 places and decimals down to many places, should have omitted to mention any measurement for determining these Swarams. They knew very well that even if there was the minutest difference in the Sa-Pa relation, other Swarams could never be derived. They put the seal of Sa-Pa and Sa-Ma on the Sapta Swarams just as weights and measures are so sealed that there might not be even the difference of a grain.

Even this seal is not measured or weighed but should be appreciated by the ear. It follows therefore, that one must possess a highly advanced musical ear so that when one has once understood the harmony of Sa-Pa, one might apply the same test to all other Swarams.

We shall see that this standard has been used in different places at different times. We shall see in many places that Swarams in a Yal were arranged on the same principle, and the same recommended: that Yals were tuned on the same principle. The Swarams from Kural, the primary Swaram, to Ili formed the Mandhara Sthayi; then they proceeded upwards from Ili as Kural. Here we find that Kural is the first Swaram of the Mandhara Sthayi, and the Ili (which was fixed as the Kural) the first Swaram of the Madhaya Sthayi. Here we shall find that the concord Sa to Ma is derived from the harmonious Sa to Pa. In the same way, we shall find that they made their Ganam with no difference between the ascending series Sa, Ri, Ga, Ma and Pa, Dha, Ni, Sa, Ri, and in descending, between Ri, Sa, Ni, Dha, Pa and Sa, Ni, Dha, Pa, Ma for all Swarams were based on the principle of Sa-Pa. This may be seen from the following extracts and the cycles which will help in the elucidation thereof.

We have noted in the first part of this book, which deals with the history of music, that Iyal, Isai and Natakam, the three Angams of the Tamil language were cultivated and brought to a highly efficient state by the members of the Sangam in South Madura about 12000 years ago. This Sangam was under the patronage of the Pandyan kings and Tamil scholars of the period who flourished in South Madura, the capital of Lemuria or the province of Kumari as it was then known. From the same source we understand that the ancients were highly proficient in music, that they generated Ragas with the help of the seven fundamental Swarams in the octave in the four different Palais—Ayapalai, Vattapali, Thirikonapalai and Chathurapalai, that they had four different kinds of Yal, with four sub-sections in each and that they used still minuter Srutis in those Ragas. The minuteness of the system which they had, suggests the fact that all ancient musical culture has now disappeared and that we have been now reduced to such a poor condition that we are groping about even in the 12 Swarams. Ayapalai is mentioned first among the four Palais. The 12 Swarams of Ayapalai and the 12 Palais which generate from them while the change of Graham is made (seven primary and five secondary) are also clearly set forth.

2. How the 14 Palais are derived from Ayapalai.

(Karunamirtha Sagaram in Tamil Page 530—533.)

"ஈரேழ் தொடுத்த செம்முறைக் கேள்வியி
னீரேழ் பாலை நிறுத்தல் வேண்டி"

என்பது. ஆயப்பாலையாய் நின்ற பதினாற்கோவை, கோவினிது செப்ப முடைத்தாய்ப் பெண்டிர்க்குரிய தான முடைய பாடலியல்பொத்தமைந்த சிறப்புடைத்தாகலான், இதிலே செம்பாலை, படுமலைப்பாலை செவ்வழிப் பாலை, அரும்பாலை, கோடிப்பாலை, விளரிப்பாலை, மேற்செம்பாலை யெனப்பட்ட வெழுபாலையினையும் இணைநரம்பு தொடுத்து நிரம்ப நிறுத்திக்காட்டல் காரணமாக வென்க.

He says here that Ayapalai is the first of the chief four Palais (1) Ayapalai (2) Thirikonapalai, (3) Chathurapalai and (4) Vattapalai.

There are two kinds, the first commences with Tharam as Kural (SA) and the other with Oolai (or MA) as Kural. Each of these is capable of seven Palais, thus accounting for the 14 Palais in all. The Swarams of these two series have the same concord with one another as SA has to PA. Their detail might be seen in the following Table. For these 14 Moorchanas, the first seven have seven names, commencing with Chempalai, and the second seven, the names beginning with Arumpalai. The Swarams of the two series are in the relation of SA to PA.

Therefore, the Kural (SA) derived from Oolai (MA) gives us the seven Palais from Chempalai.

The Oolai (MA) derived from Tharam (NI) gives us another seven Palais from Kodipalai.

Silappadikaram Venirkathai p. 202.

"பிழையா மரபி னீரேழ் கோவையை
யுழைமுதற் கைக்கிளை யிறுவாய்க் கட்டி"

(இ-ள்) மயங்கா மரபினையுடைய இப் பதினாற்கோவையாகிய சகோடயாழை உழை குரலாகக் கைக்கிளை தாரமாகக் கட்டியென்க.

(The 14 Swarams are from Ni of the Mandhara Sthayi to Dha of the Thara Sthayi).

"தாரத்துட் டோன்று முழையுழை யுட்டோன்று
மோருங் குரல்குரலி னுட்டோன்றிச்-சேருமிளி
யுட்டோன்றுந் துத்தத்துட் டோன்றும் விளரியுட்
கைக்கிளை தோன்றும் பிறப்பு"

என்பதனால் தாரத்தில் முற் பிறப்பதாகிய உழை குரலாய்க் கைக்கிளை தாரமாகிய கோடிப்பாலை முதற் பிறக்கக் கட்டி யென்க.

When Oolai becomes Kural (Ma becomes Sa) in the Sakotayal and if Ga (Kaikilai) is made Ni (Tharam) the series Ma, Pa, Dha, Ni, Sa, Ri, Ga will result.

Again, when Oolai or Ma is made into Kural or Sa the series will be Sa, Ri, Ga, Ma, Pa ,Dha, Ni.

When Ma (Oolai commences on Ni (Tharam) the series will be Ni, Sa, Ri, Ga, Ma, Pa, Dha.

The different series, then, are :—

Ni	Sa	Ri	Ga	Ma	Pa	Dha
Ma	Pa	Dha	Ni	Sa	Ri	Ga
Sa	Ri	Ga	Ma	Pa	Dha	Ni

These series will clearly demonstrate the meaning of the stanza commencing with the words "*தாரத்துட்டோன்றும் உழை* & c".

So by the Sa-Pa principle :—

Oolai	...	(Ma)	will be derived from			Tharam	(Ni)
Kural	...	(Sa)	,,	,,	,,	Oolai	(Ma)
Ili	...	(Pa)	,,	,,	,,	Kural	(Sa)
Thuttham	...	(Ri)	,,	,,	,,	Ili	(Pa)
Vilari	...	(Dha)	,,	,,	,,	Thutham	(Ri)
Kaikilai	...	(Ga)	,,	,,	,,	Vilari	(Dha)
Tharam	...	(Ni)	,,	,,	,,	Kaikilai	(Ga)

This is the meaning of the expression that Kural became Ili. The above series are all on the principle of Sa-Pa. When Oolai (or Ma) is made into Kural (or Sa), Kaikilai (or Ga) which is before Oolai (or Ma) becomes Tharam (or Ni). This he calls **Kodipalai.**

3. The Seven Palais beginning from Chempalai and how they are derived.

Number.	Ma Kural Sa	Pa Thuttham Ri	Dha Kaikilai Ga	Ni Oolai Ma	Sa Ili Pa	Ri Vilari Dha	Ga Tharam Ni	Ma Kural Sa	Pa Thuttham Ri	Dha Kaikilai Ga	Ni Oolai Ma	Sa Ili Pa	Ri Vilari Dha	Ga Tharam Ni
1	Sa	Ri	Ga	Ma	Pa	Dha	Ni	Sa						
2		Sa	Ri	Ga	Ma	Pa	Dha	Ni	Sa					
3			Sa	Ri	Ga	Ma	Pa	Dha	Ni	Sa				
4				Sa	Ri	Ga	Ma	Pa	Dha	Ni	Sa			
5					Sa	Ri	Ga	Ma	Pa	Dha	Ni	Sa		
6						Sa	Ri	Ga	Ma	Pa	Dha	Ni	Sa	
7							Sa	Ri	Ga	Ma	Pa	Dha	Ni	Sa

1	Sa	Sa	When Kural is taken as Kural	... Chempalai.
2	Ri	Sa	When Thuttham is taken as Kural	... Padumalaipalai.
3	Ga	Sa	When Kaikilai is taken as Kuaral	... Chevvalipalai.
4	Ma	Sa	When Oolai is taken as Kural	... Arumpalai.
5	Pa	Sa	When Ili is taken as Kural ...	. Kodipalai.
6	Dha	Sa	When Vilari is taken as Kural	... Vilaripalai.
7	Ni	Sa	When Tharam is taken as Kural	... Merchempalai.

In this Chakaram we have shown how the seven Palais are derived from the series MA, PA, DHA, NI, SA, RI, GA and SA, RI, GA, MA, PA, DHA, NI which are obtained by the SA-PA system taking Oolai (or MA) as the Kural (SA). When we deal later on with Vattapalai we may see how these Swarams are concordant by the SA-PA system. We must remember that when Oolai is taken as Kural, and Tharam as Oolai which in its turn is taken as Kural, they are all after the SA-PA system. When Tharam becomes Oolai and when this Oolai is taken as Kural. he calls it Kodipalai.

In the above Table, each of the seven Palais commencing from Chempalai (where Kural stands for SA) proceeds from Kural towards the right side and becomes a Moorchana. Each of these Moorchanas receives a separate name according to the Swaram from which it commences.

For example·

The	SA	which commences from	SA	is Chempalai.
The	SA	,, ,, ,,	Ri	is Padumalaipalai.
The	SA	,, ,, ,,	GA	is Chevvalipalai.
The	SA	,, ,, ,,	MA	is Arumpalai.
The	SA	,, ,, ,,	PA	is Kodipalai.
The	SA	,, ,, ,,	DHA	is Vilaripalai.
The	SA	,, ,, ,,	Ni	is Merchempalai.

These names become different in the second Chakaram. They are purposely given different names there, in as much as they occur on doubled Swarams from SA-PA. Moreover we shall see from the Tables of Palais to be given later on, that these have different names when they proceed by the SA-PA system towards the right, and by the SA-MA system towards the left. These different names depend upon the place where SA commences in the various strings of Swarams such as SA-PA, MA-SA, PA-SA, NI-MA in the four kinds of Yal. This fact may be clearly seen from the Tables below.

4. The Mandhara, Madhya and Thara Sthayis.

(Karunamirtha Sagaram in Tamil Page 535)

Silappadikaram, Arangetukathei P. 93.

"ஏனை மகளிருங் கிளைவழிச் சேர"

என்பது, இதனைப் பெண்டிர்க்குரிய தானமாகிய பதினாற்கோவையிலே பொருந்தக்கூட்ட வேண்டுமென்றவாறு கூட்டும்படி :

He says that "this should be added to the 14 Kovais which include the place for women." 80-81.

"மேல துழையிளி கீழது கைக்கிளை
வம்புறு மரபிற் செம்பாலை யாயது"

என்பது, உழை முதற் கைக்கிளை இறுதியாக மெலிவு நான்கும், சமம் ஏழும், வலிவு மூன்றுமாய் உழை முதலாக செம்பாலையாயதென்க.

He says here, there are four soft sounds from Oolai up to Kaikilai, middling sounds seven and hard sounds three.

From this we are able to conclude that when Oolai commences as the Kural, we have four Swarams up to Oolai which takes the place of Tharam (SA, RI, GA, MA) for the Mandara Sthayi (soft sounds), the seven Swarams from Oolai which takes the place of Tharam up to Kaikilai for the Madhya Sthayi (Middling sounds) and the three Swarams PA, DHA, NI above Oolai which commences in Tharam up to Tharam which commences in Kaikilai for the Thara Sthayi (hard sounds).

" வலிவு மெலிவுஞ் சமனு மெல்லாம்
போலியக் கோத்த புலமை யோனுடன் "

என்பது, இப்படியால். வலிவும் மெலிவும் சமனுமெனப்படாநின்ற தானநிலையினையுடைய இசைக்கூறு பாடுகளுக்கெல்லாம் நரப்படைவு கெடாமலும் பண்ணீர்மை முதலாயின குன்றாமலும் புணர்க்கவல்லவனாய், அப்புணர்ப்பிற் கமைந்த எழுத்துக்களால் இசை செய்ய வல்ல யாழாசிரியனுமென்றவாறு. நிறுத்தல் வேண்டிப் பொலியக் கோத்த புலமையோனென்க.

Here he says that an expert in the playing of the Yal should be one who must be able to discriminate and adjust the different hard soft and middling sounds, so that the sweet harmony of the strings and the sounds may not be impaired and who could compose music by arranging these harmonious sounds.

Melivu	Samam	Valivu
Mandharam	Madhyam	Tharam
Ni, Sa, Ri, Ga	Ma, Pa, Dha, Ni, Sa, Ri, Ga	Ma, Pa, Dha
Ma, Pa, Dha, Ni	Sa, Ri, Ga, Ma, Pa, Dha, Ni	Sa, Ri, Ga

Here we find that the four Swarams Ni, Sa, Ri and Ga of the top line belong to the lower Sthayi, the seven Swarams Ma Pa, Dha, Ni, Sa, Ri and Ga to the middle Sthayi and the three Swarams Ma, Pa and Dha to the upper Sthayi. In the bottom line the four Swarams Ma, Pa Dha and Ni as are in use at present, belong to the Mandhara Sthayi, the seven Swarams Sa, Ri, Ga, Ma, Pa, Dha and Ni to the Middle Sthayi and the three Swarams Sa, Ri and Ga to the Thara Sthayi. These are hard, soft and middling sounds.

5. The Vattapalai which was in use in Isai-Tamil.

(Karunamirtha Sagaram in Tamil Page 536—539)

From the calculations of the Vattapalai we understand that there were four Palais, Ayapalai, Chathurapalai, Thirikonapalai and Vattapalai, and that the calculation of the Srutis of each of them was also given. Looking at the calculations of the Ayapalai, we find they resemble those of the Vattapalai. But we also find that Madavi played her Sakota Yal tuning it on the principle of Sa-Pa and that this was the favourite music of women in those days. We have already noted the Sruti system of the Sakota Yal. Apart from this, he mentions how Vattapalai is arrived at, the order of its Swarams, the Srutis for each of the Swarams and the minuter Swarams derived from them; particulars about Thirikonapalai and Chathurapalai will be given later on. But we are sure that the order of the Swarams of Ayapalai and the particulars about Vattapalai are enough to determine the state of ancient South Indian music. This Vattapalai is illustrated in the form of a Rasimandalam. To those who have a knowledge of Astrology, the Saptasthanams which are arrived at by computing the Sthanams seven by seven omitting the Rasi in which the Swaram occurs, the Kandrasthanams, the Sthanams for Mathru, Putthira, Kalathira and Pithur and the use of the Swarams for the respective Sthanams will be clearly known. These have been clearly set forth in the form of Tables. If one of the Chakarams could be studied and understood the others will be quite easy. But as the matter contained in them are not in use at the present time we have thought it well to give them separately.

Silappadikaram Aychiarkuravai Page 405.

" குடமுத லிடமுறை யாக்குர ளுத்தங்
கைக்கிளை யுழையிளி விளரி தாரமென
விரிதரு பூங்குழல் வேண்டிய பெயரே "

பாலை நான்கு வகைப்படும்; ஆயப்பாலை, சதுரப்பாலை, திரிகோணப்பாலை, வட்டப்பாலையென என்னை ?

" ஆயஞ் சதுரந் திரிகோணம் வட்டமெனப்
பாய நான்கும் பாலை யாகும் "

There are four kinds of Palai :—Ayapalai, Chathurapalai, Thirikonapalai and Vattapalai.

அவற்றுள் வட்டப்பாலை வருமாறு :

" வட்ட மென்பது வகுக்குங் காலை
யோரேழ் தொடுத்த மண்டலமாகும். "

" சாணளவு கொண்ட தொருவட்டந் தன்மீது
பேணி யிருநாலு பெருந் திசைக்-கோணத்
திருகயிறு மேலோட்டி யொன்பானு மூன்றும்
வருமுறையே மண்டலத்தை வை "

என்பது சூத்திர மென்னுதலிற்றோவெனின், வட்டப்பாலை மண்டலம் வருமிடத்துச் சாணுக்குச்சாணுக ஒரு வட்டங்கீறிப் பெருந் திசைகளின்மேலே இரண்டு வரம்புகீறி மண்டலஞ்செய்து பன்னிரண்டு கோணமாக வகுப்பது நுதலிற்று.

This says that a circle must be drawn whose diameter is one Chan (about 10 inches) and it should be divided into four great sections according to the cardinal points of the compass and the four sections should be divided into 12 equal compartments.

" எதிருமி ராசி வலமிடமாக
வெதிரா விடமீன மாக-முதிராத
வீராறி ராசிகளை யிட்டடைவே நோக்கவே
யோரார்த்த மண்டலமென் றெண் "

என்பது சூத்திரம் என்னுதலிற்றோவெனின், இட்ட பன்னிரண்டு கோணத்திற் பன்னிரண்டு ராசிகளை நிறுத் தினுல் இவற்றுள் நரம்புடனியல்வன எழென்பதுணர்த்து தனுதலிற்று.

If the 12 Rasis be distributed to the 12 compartments, seven of them would indicate the seven sounds.

" ஏத்து மிடப மலவனுடன் சீயங்
கோற்றனுக் கும்பமோடு மீனமிவை-பார்த்து
துரன்முதற் றுர மிறைவாய்க் கிடந்த
நிரலேழுஞ் செம்பாலை நேர் "

இவ்வேழும் இடபம், கற்கடகம் சிங்கம், துலாம், தனு. கும்பம். மீனமென இவற்றனிற்கும்.

These seven sounds would occur on the following seven signs of the Zodiac: Idapam, Karkatakam, Simham. Thulam. Thanusu, Kumbam and Meenam,

" துலைநிலைக் குரலுந் தனுநிலைத் துத்தமு
நிலைபெற கும்பத்து நேர்கைக் கிளையு
மீனத் துழையும் விடைநிலைத் திளியு
மானக் கடகத்து மன்னிய விளரியு
மரியிடைத் தாரமு மணைவுறக் கோளலே "

This also illustrates the above. The Mathirais of these seven strings or sounds are indicated by what is quoted below.

இனி நரம்புகளின் மாத்திரைகள் வருமாறு :

" குரலத்த நான்கு கிளைமூன் றிரண்டாங்
குரையா வுழையிளி நான்கு-விரையா
விளரியெனின் மூன்றிரண்டு தாரமெனச் சொன்னார்
களரிசேர் கண்ணுற் றவர் "

எனக்கொள்க. இவற்றுள், தாரத்து உழைபிறக்கும்; உழையிற் குரல் பிறக்கும்; குரலுள் இளிபிறக்கும்; இளியுள் துத்தம் பிறக்கும்; துத்தத்துள் விளரி பிறக்கும்; விளரியுட் கைக்கிளை பிறக்குமெனக் கொள்க. இவற்றுள் முதலிற்றோன்றிய நரம்பு தாரம்; இவை விரிப்பிற் பெருகும்; வந்தவழிக் கண்டுகொள்க."

In the above he says "that Oolai generates from Taram, Kural from Oolai, Ili from Kural, Thuttham from Ili, Vilari from Thuttham and Kaikilai from Vilari. Of these the first string is Tharam ; we need not dilate on this, the others might be easily understood."

In accordance with the above Sootrams and their annotation, we may make the following Chakram and divide it into 12 compartments for the 12 signs of the Zodiac commencing with Mesham and ending with Meenam. Within these 12 compartments we should locate

Kural	(Sa)	and Ili	(Pa)	in Rishabam	or the	2nd	compartment.
Thuttham	(Ri)	and Vilari	(Dha)	in Katakam	..	4th	,,
Kaikilai	(Ga)	and Tharam	(Ni)	in Simham	,,	5th	,,
Oolai	(Ma)	and Kural	(Sa)	in Thulam	,,	7th	,,
Ili	(Pa)	and Thuttham	(Ri)	in Thanus	,,	9th	,,
Vilari	(Dha)	and Kaikilai	(Ga)	in Kumbam	,,	11th	,,
Tharam	(Ni)	and Oolai	(Ma)	in Meenam	,,	12th	,,

Of these Kural has 4 Alakus, Thuttham 4, Kaikilai 3, Oolai 2, Ili 4, Vilari 3, and Tharam 2 or in all there are 22 Alakus.

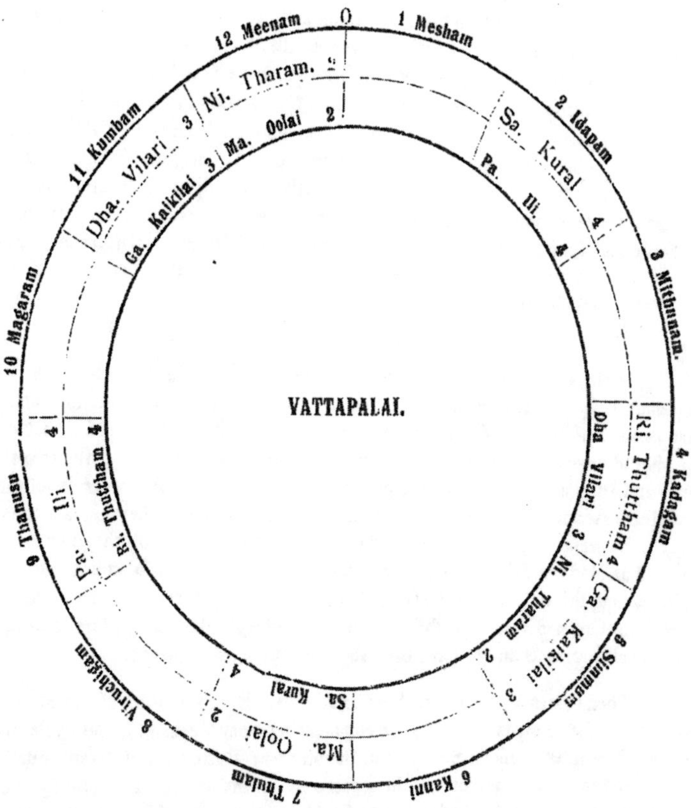

Here the author says that Oolai will be derived from Tharam, in the 12th compartment or if we take the seventh place from there, this Oolai will be derived from Thulam, that Kural will be derived from Rishabam (2nd compartment) which is the seventh place from Thulam, that Thuttham from Ili will be derived from Thanus (9th compartment) which is the seventh place from Rishabam, that Vilari from Thuttham will be derived from Kadagam which is the seventh place from Thanus, and that Kaikilai from Vilari will be derived from Kumbam which is the seventh place from Kadagam.

In the 12th compartment at the sign of Meenam, Oolai generates from Tharam and Kural from Oolai. This is the first born among sounds.

The Chakaram for Vattapalai also gives clearly the Swarams and their respective Alakus.

When we notice the Chakaram we find that Swarams occur in places which proceed by sevens. These proceed also by the SA-PA system. The first Swaram and its derived Swaram in the seventh place will stand in the relation of Kalathiram to each other. If the first Swaram be 1, the Kalathira Swaram will be 1½. If a Sthayi comes to an end on the first Swaram after a cycle, the end Swaram will be double the original Swaram, whereas a concordant Swaram will stand in the relation of 1 to 1½. The Swarams with the latter ratio will be as harmonious as the harmony between Sakti and Sivam, husband and wife. In Astrology, the seventh from the original Sthanam is considered the Kalathira Sthanam, but here as Athara Shadjam is taken to be 0, if we proceed by sevens omitting the original Sthanam we shall obtain, as in Astrology, all the Swarams of a Ragam, their relation as Chathru and Mithru, Kalathira and Puthira Mathur and Pithir and their respective uses. It will enable us to discord all the Chathuru Swarams and include the Mithru Swarams.

(Karunamirtha Sagaram in Tamil Page 577 and 578.)

In the above pages only a portion of the Isai-Tamil practised by the ancient Tamilians is seen. It is clearly seen that the three octaves, soft, middling and hard)Mandhara, Madhya and Thara) proceed upwards in the ratio of 1, 2 and 4, that a musician should have a well-trained ear to appreciate the perfect harmony of the two strings Kural and Ili in accordance with the *pun* to be sung and that the Swarams of the Yal should be determined by the SA-PA system. It is also seen that their Ganam consisted of seven Swarams (from MA to GA) which are in the middle of the fourteen thus obtained as Madhya Sthayi, the four Swarams from SA to MA as Mandira Sthayi and the remaining three Swarams RI, GA and MA as Thara Sthayi, and that they sang Ragas with Graha Swarams in them. This is called Ayapalai. It appears to have been sung in half Swarams and to have been the favourite mode of women.

Then comes Vattapalai with its 22 Alakus. Here the order of the Swarams is indicated by the 12 signs of the Zodiac commencing from Mesham. This cycle indicates the different harmonious Swarams in the different Rasis with different number of Alakus, and that the Swarams should proceed by sevens on the right side by the SA-PA system and by fives on the left by the SA-MA system. In addition to that, it shows how the Alakus should occur on the right side and on the left, when the change of Grahaswarams takes place. The seven primary Palais and the five secondary ones which are derived from the 12 Palais are also indicated. The four kinds of Yal, Marutham, Kurinchi, Neythal and Palai which generate from the four Swarams of the seven primary Palais namely SA, MA, PA and Ni are also given there. In each of these, the *puns* derived from Swarams SA, GA, PA and NI are divided into four divisions, namely, Ahanilai, Puranilai, Arugial and Perugial. The system of Alakus for each of them, the order of their Swarams and names are also indicated. The seven *puns* which are derived from each of these 16 sub-divisions may also be seen there.

When we observe these things more minutely, we are led to say that the chief *amsams* of Srutis, their system of change of Graham and the system of deriving Ragas from them are of a superior order. It is also clear that every Ragam had 22 Alakus.

When we made an attempt to get at the names of the Ragas used after the particular system and their Swarams in Aroganam and Avaroganam we came across the Swarams for the 16 *puns* pertaining to the four *yals* and their system of Alakus. From this we get the order of Swarams of the 112 *puns*, but we are at a loss to specity the special *puns* for which the special Swarams are used. However, we have to congratulate ourselves, that we have been furnished with so much musical information while the story of Kovalan was given. We come across the conflicting opinions of the commentators here and there. This only goes to prove that there were many superior *amsams* of music in the Isai-Tamil of ancient India. We have only reproduced the general indisputable opinions that may be gathered from the annotations. Some of the subtle points which are like sealed book will be noted later on.

Our readers will naturally be inquisitive to know whether the ancient Tamils were so advanced in Isai-Tamil, whether there were four kinds of Yal at the time and the rules for playing them. We shall see from the extracts that follow and from the rules given there, that their knowledge of Srutis and their trained ear to appreciate and understand their harmony were only in proportion to their practical knowledge in producing sweet and harmonious sounds from those instruments.

Beloved readers! though it is impossible to understand completely the different kinds of Yals and the Ragas used by the ancient Tamilians, we have quoted here a few Sootrams from Silappadikaram which are helpful in understanding them to a certain extent. Still more minute *amsams* as regards Isai-Tamil will be found in the same book. Though a few points as regards Isai-Tamil are found here and there in Tamil works which came after Silappadikaram, yet, as they do not treat about Srutis which are the basis of all music, nor about the generation of Ragas, nor about the change of Graha Swarams nor about Alakus but treat about some well known general points we have not thought it worth while to quote them here. Ilankovadigal, the author of Silappadikaram, has treated about some of the important *amsams* of music in his work. His commentators have done their best to throw light upon his work with the help of treatises on Isai-Tamil which were very rarely in use at the time. But in many places they have just indicated the headings of stanzas and have filled the rest with dots only. But for this we should be in a position to understand many things which existed at the first Ooli.

During the reign of Nilandarutheruvil Pandya, who was ruling in South Madura (or the destroyed Lemuria) at the close of the first Ooli there was a Sangam of scholars which had been in existence for 4400 years. Athankotasan, one of the disciples of Agastya, was one of the scholars of the Sangam before whom the well known work or grammar, namely, Tholkappiam, was presented and recited for approval. Here, in the chapter on Ahaporul, where the author speaks of the grains pertaining to the four different kinds of soil, he gives four kinds of *yal* for the four kinds of soil. Ilankovadigal shows how the four kinds of *yal* generate from Vattapalai and adds how the four Jatis are derived from them and also mentions many other important *amsams* in connection thereof. Jayankondan, the prince of poets, who lived long after Ilankovadigal, and Adyarkunallar have written about many interesting points as regards Isai-Tamil in their commentaries on the same. We clearly see that the modern Karnatic Ganam is quite in accordance with the points about Isai-Tamil mentioned by them, but that the Ganam is gradually deteriorating by the introduction of Desikam by those who have no trained ear for music. The exalted state of Isai-Tamil for nearly 1200 years is clearly seen here. We think it necessary that we should know some of the implied mysteries of this work and also the Kalais of Isai-Tamil which were in use then. However, as it is only of secondary importance in a treatise on Srutis which is our main subject, we have dealt with it only in a casual way and quoted only a few Sootrams here and there with their respective annotations. Those who want to know the minute details of the subject may do well to study Silappadikaram.

6. The method of finding out concordant Swarams.

(Karunamirtha Sagaram in Tamil Page 651—652.)

We have already seen the extent of the field of South Indian music and the system of music in which the Swarams are determined by the SA-PA and SA-MA principle. Writers have clearly showed the Swarams which will be in perfect concord with one another, and the Swarams that will be discordant. One reason for the excellence of Indian music is the regularity with which these Swarams concord with one another and their special charm when separately and independently used.

Silappadikaram, Venirkadai Page. 202.

" இணைகிளை பகைநட் பென்றிந் நான்கி
னிசைபுணர் குறிநிலை யெய்த நோக்கி"

இணை கிளை பகை நட்பென்று சொல்லப்பட்ட நான்கினும் இணை-இரண்டு நரம்பு; என்னை?

Comment. There are four different kinds of Swarams இணை or harmonious, கிளை or branch, பகை or enmity நட்பு or friendship. Of these இணை has two strings What are they ?

" இணை யெனப்படுவ கீழு மேலு
மணையத் தோன்று மளவினவென்ப"

Comment. The இணை or harmonious strings are those which appear above and below a Swaram with a particular measurement.

Silappadikaram Arumpathavurai Page. 31.

"வரன் முறையாவது முன் கூறின வகையே ஐந்தா நரம்பா முறைமையின், இளிகுரலாக ஏழு நரம்பும் வாசித்தாளென்க. குரல் குரலாகவும் குரல் தாரமாகவும் வாசித்தாளென்றவாறு.

Comment. The relation of Varan or husband is the fifth string. It implies she played on all the seven strings having Kural for Ili. It also implies that she played. Kural as Kural and as Taram.

The பகை or enmity strings are the Sixth and the third.

பகை ஆறும் மூன்றும்,

'நின்ற நரம்பிற் காறு மூன்றுஞ்
சென்று பெற நிற்பது கூடமாகும்"

கூடமெனினும் பகையெனினு மொக்கும். நட்பு நாலா நரம்பு.

*இணை ஐந்தா நரம்பென்றும் பகை ஆறு நரம்பென்றும் பிரதிபேதமுண்டு.

கூடம் and பகை are the same. The நட்பு or string for friendship is the fourth

It is also held that கிளை (or branch) is the fifth string and பகை (or enmity) is the sixth string.

The above extracts show that when Ragas were sung in ancient times indicating Kalam. Paruvam, Samayam and Porul with a view to produce a perfect concord among the known Swarams, four distinct and important varieties of Swa ams, relative Swarams, branch Swarams, discordant or enmity Swarams and friendship Swarams, were duly observed.

(Karunamirtha Sagaram in Tamil Page 824 and 825)

However, in the Chakaram given below, we see how in an octave the 12 Swarams of Ayapalai generate, commencing from Kural in the Idapam, the second Rasi, proceeding by sevens on the right side, having Ili for Kural, by the Sa-Pa series and by the concordant Swarams. Here each Rasi has two Alakus. This is mentioned here so that we may easily make the calculations for the Swarams in use at the modern day. But we must reckon that Kural and Ili occur in single Rasis and the other five in double Rasis.

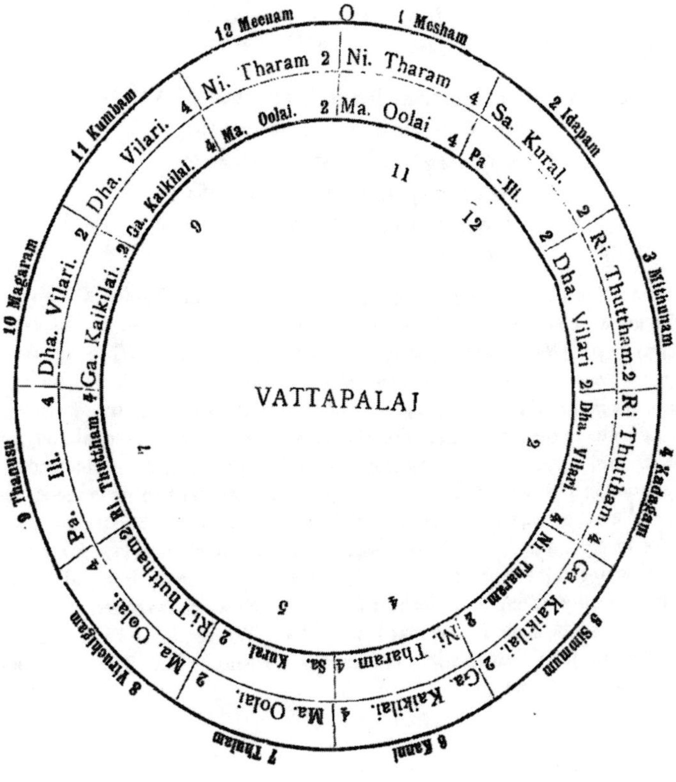

The 12 Swarams derived from Vattapalai by the Sa-Pa systems while proceeding on the right.

Ili in Kural...	SA2 PA2	Thuttham in Oolai	MA4 R12
Thuttham in Ili	PA2 R14	Vilari in Thuttham...	R12 DA2
Vilari in Thuttham	R14 DA4	Kaikilai in Vilari	DA2 GA2
Kaikilai in Vilari	DA4 GA4	Tharam in Kaikilai	GA2 N12
Tharam in Kaikilai	GA4 N14	Oolai in Tharam	N12 MA2
Oolai in Tharam	N14 MA4	Kural in Oolai	MA2 SA2

The 12 Swarams derived from Vattapalai by the Sa-Ma system while proceeding on the left.

Kural in Oolai	MA2 SA2	Oolai in Tharam...	N14 MA4
Ili in Kural	SA2 PA2	Thuttham in Oolai...	MA4 R12
Thuttham in Ili	PA2 R14	Vilari in Thuttham	R12 DA2
Vilari in Thuttham...	R14 DA4	Kaikilai in Vilari	DA2 GA2
Kaikilai in Vilari	DA4 GA4	Tharam in Kaikilai	GA2 N12
Tharam in Kaikilai	GA4 N14	Oolai in Tharam	N12 MA2

7. The Swarams from which the four kinds of Yal generate.

(Karunamirtha Sagaram in Tamil Page 726 and 727)

"தாரத் துழைதோன்ற பாலையாழ் தண்குர
லோருழைத் தோன்ற குறிஞ்சியாழ்-நேரே
இளிகுரலிற் றோன்றி மருதயாழ் துத்த
மிளியிற் பிறக்கநெய்தல் யாழ்."

Here he says that Palai Yal is obtained when Oolai appears in Tharam, Kurinji Yal is obtained when Oolai appears in Kural, Marutha Yal is obtained when Ili appears in Kural and Neythal Yal is obtained when Thuttham appears in Ili. When we observe this system more minutely, we find that Palai Yal generates from the Thara string which stands in the relation of string of friendship to the standard string, when we obtain 24 Srutis in the octave after once the mystery has been cleared, although we have mentioned in the Vattapalai system given before, that Palai Yal is obtained when Oolai appears in Tharam (N12 MA2). The tenth to the standard string is the string of enmity. We see by various means that Palai Yal never occurs in the string of enmity but in the string of friendship. In the system of Vattapalai given below, MA whiah is the branch string to the string taken as the standard commencing from Idapam, PA which is the relative string to the standard string and NI which is the string of friendship to PA should be taken for the four kinds of Yal. We mentioned before that Palai-yal will generate from Tharam which is the striug of enmity to PA. This is the hidden mystery which is now solved.

The system with the mystery removed in connection with the four kinds of Yal.

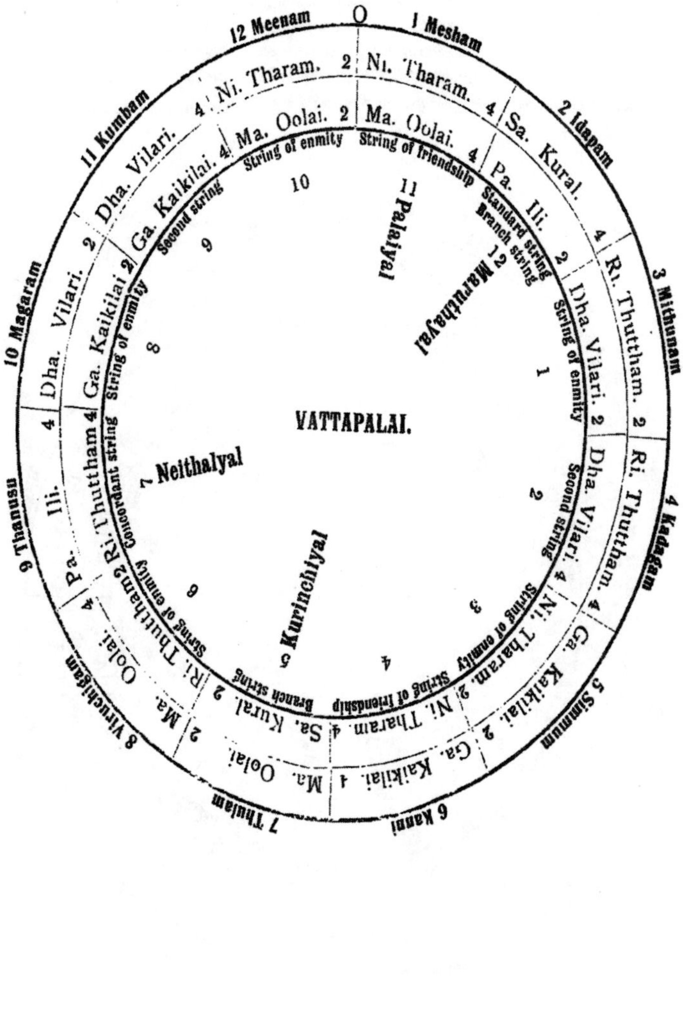

8. How the four Jathis generate from each Yal when once the mystery has been cleared.

(Karunamirtha Sagaram in Tamil Page 728—729.)

It has become a necessity to consider once more the four Jathis, Ahanilai, Puranilai, Arugial and Perugial derived from the four kinds of Yal mentioned in the previous Chakaram.

Silappadikaram Venirkathai P. 203.

" உழைமுத லாகவு முழையீறாகவுங்
குரன்முத லாகவுங் குரலீ றாகவு
மகநிலை மருதமும் புறநிலை மருதமு
மருகியன் மருதமும் பெருகியன் மருதமு
நால்வகைச் சாதியு நலம்பெற நோக்கி "

இனி உழை குரன் முதல் குரலீறாயுள்ள நான்கிற்கும் அகநிலை மருத முதற் பெருகியன் மருதம் ஈறாயுள்ள நான்கும் திரனிறை ;

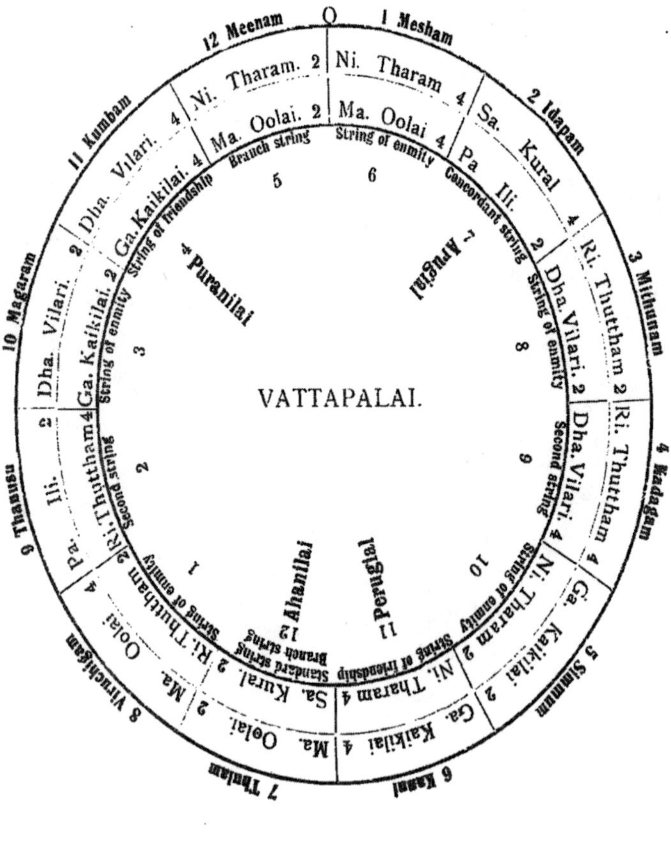

Commentary.— The four strings commencing from Oolai and Kural and ending with Kural form the Aganilai Marutham. . In the same manner the Kodipalai where Oolai becomes Kural is Aganilai Marutham; the Merchempalai with Oolai as Kural and Kaikilai as Kural is Puranilai Marutham; the Chempalai with Kural taken as Kural is Arugial Marutham; and Vilaripalai with Kural as Tharam and Tharam as Kural is Perugial Marutham. All these Jathis have harmonious Swarams.

He first makes mention of the four kinds of Yal obtained in the following manner:—

When Oolai is first and last, or in other words to have the Kural that appears in Thulam as the first and last, is one; to have the Kural that appears in Idapam as first and last is another; to have the Thuttham that appears in Thanusu as first (Kural) and last is a third, and to have the Oolai as first (Kural) and last that appears in Mesham is the fourth Yal. Then he proceeds to mention the four Jathis which are the sub-sections of the four kinds of Yal. He gives the name of Kodipalai to the Kural that appears in Thulam. The seven concordant Swarams derived from Kodipalai are the Aganilai Marutham.

If we commence Kural from Kaikilai, which is the fourth string from the Kural that appears in Thulam, we obtain Puranilai Marutham. These are friendly Swarams of the Sa-Ga type.

When Kural which appears in Oolai is taken as Kural we get Arugial Marutham. These are concordant Swarams of the Sa-Pa type.

Going onwards when Kural becomes Tharam and *vice versa* it is Perugial Marutham. When he says "while Kural becomes Tharam" it means while Kural is Kural or the first and last Swaram and the commencing Kural is Ni; this is Perugial. Proceeding further, he says that Ga which is the 'friendly' string to Sa (the standard string), Pa which is 'concordant' with Sa and Ni the 'friendly' string to the 'concordant' string are the Swarams where all Jathis commence. The ancient Tamilians seem to have used these 16 Jathis derived from the four kinds of Yal. They may be clearly seen in the Chakaram.

There is reason to think that ganam under this system and the Ragas derived from them were held in high esteem by the ancient Tamilians. We are at a loss to know what further subtle principles they had in use. However, I think we shall do well to see the use of the four different kinds of Yal—Palai, Kurinji, Marutham and Neythal.

9. How according to the Dwavimsati Srutis of Sarnga Dev the Vadi and Samvadi Swarams will never obtain the right measurements.

(Karunamirtha Sagaram in Tamil Page. 677—678.)

We notice here also the same defect which we pointed out as regards the Chakaram of Vattapalai, that the Alakus there do not occur with proper measurements. The system of Alakus in the order of 4, 3, 2, 4, 4, 3, 2, resembles that of Neythal Yal which is obtained when Ili is taken as Kural in the Thanusu Rasi in Vattapalai. This becomes the Ili for the Kural that appears in Idapam. We have noticed already how the 14 Kovais were sung with the Swarams from Kural to Ili as Mandhara Sthayi, from

Ili in Thanusu up to Oolai in Thulam as Madhya Sthayi and the Swarams from Ili to Meenam as Thara Sthayi. This appears to be the Panchama Sruti. This is used so even at the present day. Sarnga Dev takes this as Shadja Gramam and gives Alakus. He also calls the Swarams of Neythal Yal in Vattapalai, namely, PA^4, DHA^3, NI^2, SA^4, RI^4, GA^3 and MA^2 and their Alakus, Shadja Gramam. We must consider it a great coincidence that at least Sarnga Dev concurs with the Alakus of a Yal in Vattapalai. We must conclude that during the time of Sarnga Dev the Alaku system of Vattapalai and its Yals must have become obsolete. The Alaku system he gives is mentioned below.

1	Thuttham will appear	in Ili ...	... Pa^4-Ri^3	Pa	Dha^3	Ni^2	Sa^4	Ri^3	12
2	Vilari ,,	in Thuttham	... Ri^3-Dha^3	Ri	Ga^2	Ma^4	Pa^4	Dha^3	13
3	Kaikilai ,,	in Vilari ...	... Dha^3.Ga^2	Dha	Ni^2	Sa^4	Ri^3	Ga^2	11
4	Tharam ,,	in Kaikilai	... Ga^2-Ni^2	Ga	Ma^4	Pa^4	Dha^3	Ni^2	13
5	Oolai ,,	in Tharam	... Ni^2-Ma^2	Ni	Sa^4	Ri^3	Ga^2	Ma^4	13
6	Kural ,,	in Oolai ...	... Ma^2-Sa^4	Ma	Pa^4	Dha^3	Ni^2	Sa^4	13
7	Ili ,,	in Kural ...	... Sa^4-Pa^4	Sa	Ri^3	Ga^2	Ma^4	Pa^4	13

Here we find that the concordant Swarams PA RI, RI DHA, DHA GA, GA NI, NI MA, MA SA and SA PA are obtained as Vadi and Sam Vadi just as, according to the system of Vattapalai, we get Thuttham In Ili, Vilari in Thuttham &c. Each of these must have 13 Srutis. On the other hand, the first couple PA RI have 12 Swarams, and the third DHA GA has 11. Is it correct to have 12 and 11 Swarams, when we ought to get the number 13 all through? If Sarnga Dev was quite sure of the Srutis, will he not have explained the incongruity? He has clearly stated that if 12 Alakus and 8 Alakus occur in the midst of 2 Swarams, they stand in the relation of Vadi and Samvadi. How could a series which has 10 and 11 Srutis, omitting the first and last, be accurate and uniform? We see that such a Thuttham and Kaikilai are found in Aroganam and Avaroganam in the calculations of Alakus. It is clear that this system has been written without understanding the secret of the Vattapalai which the ancient Tamilians used.

It appears that the ancient Tamilians used ganam with seven Swarams in the 12 Palais with the 12 Rasis, and had the concordant string as the 7th in Vattapalai, the inimical string as the 6th, the branch string at the 5th and the friendly string as the 4th. They have given 22 as the number of Alakus, being at the same time cognisant of the secret contained therein. On the other hand, Sarnga Dev has erred in giving 22 Srutis in the octave not knowing the secret of the Alakus.

(Karunamirtha Sagaram in Tamil Page. 822)

The Table showing the position of the seven primary Puns derived from Chempalai in the 12 Rasis, with their respective intervals.

Six Mother Ragas.	Change of Graham of Swarams.	Beginning Swaram.	Standard string.	Second string.	String of friendship.	Branch string.	Concordant string.	Second string.	Branch string.	Ancient Tamil names.	Modern names.
			12	2	4	5	7	9	11		
			ச Sa	ரி Ri	க Ga	ம Ma	ப Pa	த Dha	நி Ni		
1	When Kural is taken as Kural.	ச Sa	1	2	2	1	2	2	2	Chempalai Pun.	Dhira Sankara-paranam.
2	When Thutham is taken as Kural.	ரி Ri	2	2	1	2	2	2	1	Padumalaipalai Pun.	Karakarapriya.
3	When Kaikilai is taken as Kural.	க Ga	2	1	2	2	2	1	2	Chevvali Pun.	Hanumat Thodi.
4	When Oolai is taken as Kural	ம Ma	1	2	2	2	1	2	2	Arumpalai Pun.	Kalyani.
5	When Ili is taken as Kural ...	ப Pa	2	2	2	1	2	2	1	Kodipalai Pun.	Harikambothi.
6	When Vilari is taken as Kural.	த Dha	2	2	1	2	2	1	2	Vilari Pun.	Nata Bayravi.
[illegible]	When Tharam is taken as Kural.	நி Ni	2	1	2	2	0	2	2	Merchempalai Pun.	Suddha Thodi.

(Karunamirtha Sagaram in Tamil Page. 823)

The Table showing the intervals of the Swarams belonging to the six mother Ragas which result from the change of Graham of Chempalai Pun or Shankaraparanam.

	Standard string. 0				Second string. 2				String of friendship. 4		Branch string. 5				Concordant string. 7				Second string. 9				String of friendship. 11		Branch string. 12	Modern system.									
	24	1	2	3	4	5	6	7	8	9	10	11	12	13	14	15	16	17	18	19	20	21	22	23	24	Modern Ragas.	The Swaram for Ragas.								
	S		R^2		R^4		G^2		G_4		M^2		M^4		P		D_2		D^4		N^2		N^4		S										
1	S				R^4				G^4		M^2				P				D^4				N^4			Sankraparanam	S	4^R	4^G	2^M	P	4^D	4^N	S	29
2	N^2				S				R^4		G^2				M^2				P				D^4			Karakarapiriya	S	4^R	2^G	2^M	P	4^D	2^N	S	22
3	D^2				N^2				S		R_2				G^2				M^2				P			HanumatThodi	S	2^R	2^G	2^M	P	2^D	2^N	S	8
4	P				D^4				N^4		S				R^4				G^4				M^4			Mecha Kalyani.	S	4^R	4^G	4^M	P	4^D	4^N	S	65
5	M^2				P				D^4		N^2				S				R^4				G^4			Harikambothi.	S	4^R	4^G	2^M	P	4^D	2^N	S	28
6	G^2				M^2				P		D^2				$N^?$				S				R^4			Nata Bairavi...	S	4^R	2^G	2^M	P	2^D	2^N	S	20
7	R^2				G^2				M^2		M^4 P^*				D^2				N_2				S			Suddha Thodi.	S	2^R	2^G	2^M		2^D	2^N	S	8

It is clearly seen from the above Table that the primary Ragam is Chempalai-pun, that it was sung in Swarasthanams 1, 2, 2, 1, 2, 2, 2, that it is known as Shankara-paranam in modern music and that the calculation of intervals for the Swarams of Ragams should be in accordance with what is given for this. Just as the seven Swarams of the standard string, second string, friendly string, branch string, concordant string and then again of the second string, friendly string and branch string occur in the 12th, the 2nd, the 4th, the 5th, the 7th, the 9th and 11th Rasis for the Chempalai Pun, it must occur for the others also. So Chempalai Pun primarily sets forth the common rule for all. Because the other six mother Ragas are formed after this system, this might be called the mother of all mother Ragas. The details of these are given in the 3rd part where we treat about the system of Yal with all mysteries cleared.

10. The calculation of the 12 Swarams that occur in Ayapalai which is found in works on Isai-Tamil.

(Karunamirtha Sagaram in Tamil Page 829—833.)

We have hitherto noted clearly the seven Swarams which were in use in Isai-Tamil, and the 12 Swarams of Ayapalai which are derived in the 12 Rasis by arranging them in the concordant string, branch string, inimical string, friendly string and the second string. We have also noted how the 12 Swarams of the octave are obtained by the SA-PA system (concordant series) in the Vattapalai Chakaram proceeding by the right and how the same are obtained (branch series) by the SA-MA system proceeding by the left.

We have also stated before, (in the Tamil book p. 822 and 823) the intervals of the six mother Ragas and their modern names and we have given the 12 Swarams obtained by proceeding on the right by the order of Kural, Ili &c., and their respective Alakus. In the same manner, the 12 Swarams obtained while proceeding on the left by the order of Oolai, Kural &c., and their respective Alakus are also given (in the Tamil book page 825).

I think that all men with knowledge of music will accept that these are the 12 Swarams that are in use in Karnatic music at the present day. These 12 Swarams are not an innovation but what have been in use under the Ayapalai and Vattapalai systems among the Tamilians for many thousand years, even before the age of the First Sangam.

There is reason to think that the 12 Swarams of the Ayapalai used in ancient times in the South Tamil country were carried to many places and adopted with slight modifications. This we have to emphasise in spite of the fact, that when Lemuria was submerged, the remnants of the Tamilians went and settled in the lands opposite to them, and that though they appeared to be different races with different colours and languages owing to peculiarities of the climate and the natural surroundings of their new homes, yet from the Tamil words found mixed in their new languages and the 12 Swarams which they had been using in music, it is established without doubt that they came from a common stock.

It appears that the knowledge of the 12 Swarams which was kept up for many thousand years mainly by a well-developed ear for music, must have varied here and there slightly. Then came the new measurement of Pythagoras 2500 years ago, when he fixed $\frac{2}{3}$ of a string for Sa-Pa and $\frac{3}{4}$ of it for Sa-Ma. Though these Swarams may be approximately correct when taken by themselves, yet when fixed as the standard, and multiplied many times over, the result does not tally with the measurements of many well-known resultant Swarams.

To add to this, the theory of Sarnga Dev, advocating 22 Srutis in the octave, gave room to many doubts As it is very necessary to clear these doubts, I have treated about them in part II.

It is necessary to understand the calculations of the 12 Swarams of Ayapalai before entering into the Swarams and minuter Srutis of Indian Music.

We have noted already that the measurement of the Sthayis given in ancient Isai-Tamil, how if Athara Sa be 1, Madhya Sa should be 2 and the end Sa of the Tara Sthayi should be 4, concurs with Sarnga Dev's measurement for the Sthayis. We must examine how the Sthayis proceed upwards in the ratio of 1, 2 and 4 producing a gradually ascending series of 12 Swarams without admitting any other possible sound in the middle.

When we take Kural to be the end Swaram or standard Swaram in the three Sthayis, low, middling and high, the seven Swarams which follow, namely, Thuttham, Kaikilai, Oolai, Ili, Vilari, Tharam and Kural, become 12 Swarams in the 12 Rasis. We have noted this already. Here the commencing Swaram should be calculated from Idapam and the last Swaram should be Kural. When we follow this calculation, if the Sa below the Mandara Sthayi be $\frac{1}{2}$, the finishing Sa of the same will be 1, if the ending Sa of the Mandhara Sthayi be 1, the ending Sa of the Madhya Sthayi will be 2. If the ending Sa of Madhya Sthayi be 2, the ending Sa of Tara Sthayi will be 4.

In all the three Sthayis the progression of the series of Swarams should be uniform. For, commencing from Athara Sa or 1, the 12 Swarams should ascend gradually with equal intervals without admitting any other possible Swaram in the middle. The end Swaram which is 2 will be the Madhya Sa. How we proceed from 1, the Athara Sa, to 2, the Madhya Sa, is shown in the Table in the next page.

The calculations to show that the Swarams used by the ancient Tamilians in Ayapalai are the ones used at present in Karnatic music.

Number.	Rasi.	Names of Srutis And Alakus.	How the 12 Swarams proceed gradually upwards from 1 to 2, by powers of $\sqrt[12]{2}$	The logarithm of the powers of $\sqrt[12]{2}$	The Anti-logarithms for the numbers in col. 4.	Vibrations of each Swaram if SA=540	Vibrations of each Swaram if SA=240	The location of the 12 Swarams in the first half of the whole string.	The position of the Swarams in a wire 32 inches long.	Measurement by inches of the Swara Sthanams while proceeding upwards from Athara SA.	The intervals (in length) between Swarams.	The cents of Ellis for the 12 Swarams
1	2		3	4	5	6	7	8	9	10	11	12
0	Idabam	S	$(\sqrt[12]{2})^0$	·000000000	1·000000	540·00	240·00	1·0000000	32·0000	0		0
1	Midunam	R_2	$(\sqrt[12]{2})^1$	·025085833	1·059463	572.11	254·28	0·9438743	30·2040	1·7960	1·7960	100
2	Kadagam	R_1	$(\sqrt[12]{2})^2$	·050171667	1·122462	606·13	269·40	0·8908986	28·5088	3·4912	1·6952	200
3	Simmum	G_2	$(\sqrt[12]{2})^3$	·075257500	1·189207	642·17	285·41	0·8408963	26·9087	5·0913	1·6001	300
4	Kanni	G_1	$(\sqrt[12]{2})^4$	·100343333	1·259921	680·36	302·38	0·7937005	25·3984	6·6016	1·5103	400
5	Thulam	M_2	$(\sqrt[12]{2})^5$	·125429167	1·334840	720·81	320·36	0·7491535	23·9729	8·0271	1·4255	500
6	Viruchigam	M_1	$(\sqrt[12]{2})^6$	·150515000	1·414214	763·68	339·41	0·7071069	22·6274	9·3726	1·3455	600
7	Thanusu	P_2	$(\sqrt[12]{2})^7$	·175600833	1·498307	809·09	359·50	0·6674199	21·3574	10·6426	1·2700	700
8	Magaram	D_2	$(\sqrt[12]{2})^8$	·200686667	1·587401	857·20	380·98	0·6299601	20·1587	11·8413	1·1987	800
9	Kumbam	D_1	$(\sqrt[12]{2})^9$	·225772500	1·681793	908·17	403·63	0·5946036	19·0273	12·9727	1·1314	900
10	Meenam	N_2	$(\sqrt[12]{2})^{10}$	·250858333	1·781797	962·17	427·63	0·5612309	17·9594	14·0406	1·0679	1000
11	Medam	N_1	$(\sqrt[12]{2})^{11}$	·275944167	1·887749	1019·38	453·05	0·5297315	16·9514	15·0486	1·0080	1100
12	Idabam	S_2	$(\sqrt[12]{2})^{12}$	·301030000	2·000000	1080·00	480·00	0·5000000	16·0000	16·0000	0·9514	1200

The logarithm of 1 is 0· The logarithm of 2 is ·301030000. These may be seen in Chamber's Mathematical Tables in the first and second lines in page 2. If this ·301030000 be divided by 12 we get ·025085833 which is the logarithm of the first of the 12 Swarams (which have 2 for their number). If this be multiplied by 2, we get the logarithm for the second Swaram, and if multiplied by 3 we get the logarithm for the third Swaram and so on. The logarithms of all the 12 Swarams are obtained in this manner. These are found in Col 4 of the above Table.

The logarithm of 2 has been divided by 12 and multiplied in order by the numbers 1 to 12. This is given in col. 3. The second column gives the Alakus for the 12 Swarams in the 12 Sthanams with their respective Rasis.

If we notice the numbers of the logarithms for the 12 Swarams we fiind ·0000000000 to be 1. The 12th logarithm ·301030000 gets 2. The fourth column gives the root numbers of the 12 Swarasthanams of the Sthayi progressing fron 1 to 2. In the same way the numbers of the 12 Swarasthanams from 1 to 2 should be noted.

The 5th column indicates the measurements of the 12 Swarams in the octave if Athara Sa be 1 and the end Sa of the Madhya Sthayi be 2. These proceed in geometrical progression. The fixed number is 2. The twelve logarithms of 2 are mentioned in Col. 4 The numbers for the logarithms in Col. 4 are given in Col. 5.

We find, then, that this is the opinion of the ancient Tamilians, that this is the system of Vattapalai and the one advocated by Sarnga Dev. This is the measurement of the natural series. Having this as the basis, we may determine the vibrations and the position of the Swarams in the wire. The measurements have been calculated down to several places of decimals so that they may be minute and at the same time accurate without causing any doubt. To examine only two or three places of decimals may be easy, but there is a chance of the calculations causing doubt if we stop there. So We request those who are earnest about it, to examine the calculations down to four places at least.

The calculation of vibrations of the 12 Swarams of Ayapalai.

(Karunamirtha Sagaram in Tamil Page 536—539)

We noticed how the series of 12 Swarams in the octave prodeeded gradually upwards from 1 to 2 according to the established rule if Athara Sa be 1, Madhya Sthayi Sa is 2. Now we should note how we obtain the vibrations for the 12 Swarams found in Col. 5. I have stated in my Tamil book of Part IV, p. 802-809 that if we suppose Athara Sa to have 540 vibrations per second, then Madhya Sa will have double or 1080 vibrations and Tara Sa will have 2160 vibrations or double that of Madhya Sa and that this is in conformity with the breath of man and the sound of the Yal. We see in column 6 of the Table how the upward progression of 540 vibrations to 1080 is a gradually ascending series of 12 steps from Athara Sa to Madhya Sa and from Madhya Sa to Thara Sa.

We see from col. 5 that the logarithm of o is 1·000000. When we multiply this by 540 we get 540. This is the number of vibrations for Athara Sa. If we multiply 1·059463, the anti-logarithm (of 1) in Col. 5 by 540 we get 572·11, and if 1·122462 the anti-logarithm (of 2) in col. 5 by 540. we obtain 606·13. In the same way if the anti-logarithms given in col. 5 in all the 12 lines be multiplied by 540, we get the vibrations of all the 12 Swarams. These are given in col. 6.

I have given the vibrations for the 12 Swarams in col. 7 supposing Athara Sa to be 240. as this measurement is advocated by some writers. We should proceed to find out the position of the 12 Swarams in a wire 32 inches long.

The location of the 12 Swarams in the exact half of a wire 32 inches long where the Madhya Sthayi ends.

The number 1 seen at the top of col. 8 of the above Table is the length of the wire. The Madhya Sa occurs exactly in the middle of this length, and Tara Sa is located in exactly a quarter of this length. The number 1 which is found in col. 5 is the number for the logarithm o in col. 4. The product of the numbers found in cols. 5 and 8 is always 1. The numbers in col. 5 found opposite the Swarams of the 12 places when multiplied by 1, give us the measurements of the 12 Swarasthanams found in col. 8.

The ·5 which is obtained for the 12th place or Sa of the Madhya Sthayi is half of the Athara Sa. The Sthanams for the 12 Swarams are found in col. 8. We should next see the places where they occur in a wire 32 inches long with the same measurements.

The measurements of the Swarams up to Madhya Sa in a wire 32 inches long.

We noted in col. 8 that if the whole length of the wire be 1, the Madhya Sthayi Sa occurs exactly at the middle of the whole length. I have also mentioned in pages 785 to 792 in my Tamil book part IV, how the Yal resembled the human body. The distance from the centre of the brew to the Moolatharam is 48 (or 47½) inches. This should be divided into 4 equal parts of a *chan* (or nearly a foot) each. Of these the distance of 3 *chans* is the place for Swarams and the remaining space is left vacant. I have there pointed out the relation between the measurement of the Sthoola Sareeram according to the measurement of the human hand and the distance of Swarams in the Yal. According to this measurement the Athara Sa will sound at the 16th inch or half the length of the wire which is 32 inches long from the Meru to the Mettu. The Madhya Sthayi Sa sounds at the 16th inch from Meru. We must see how these 12 Swarams ascend gradually from the Meru up to the 16th inch.

If each of the measurements of the 12 Swarams (given in col. 8) which proceed from 1 to ½ be multiplied by 32 we get the measurements for the 12 Swarams given in col. 9. We see that the 12th Swaram or Madhya Sthayi Sa is located exactly at the 16th inch in a wire 32 inches long.

The 10th column gives the intervals of each of the 12 Swarams beginning from the Meru and ending at the 16th inch. These measurements of the Swarasthanans are obtained by subtracting the measurements given in col. 9 from the wire 32 inches long.

The table also shows how the 12 Swarams gradually increase in pitch up to the Madhya Sthayi SA (found in line 12) and come to an end at the 16th inch of the wire whose total tength is 32 inches.

Col. 11 gives the length of wire of the intervals between Swara Sthanams. The difference of the intervals is shown here. We see, then, that the 12 Mettus of the Yal gradually decrease in intervals but increase in pitch in conformity with the natural growth of the human spine.

The cents calculation for the 12 Swarams.

The 12th column gives the cents measurements Here the Sthayi is divided into 1200 cents. There is a regular and uniform progression in the number of cents also. This shows that the Sruti system of Sarnga Dev which speaks of the 12 Swarams as a gradually ascending series without admitting any other Swaram in the middle and the system of Ayapalai of the ancient Tamilians by the SA-PA and the SA-MA principles are quite correct. The 12th col. gives the cents which anybody could easily understand.

In all the 12 columns of the above Table, I have given the calculations, the number of vibrations, the length of wire and the cents corresponding to the 12 Swarams of the octave.

I think that this system is the one where the minuteness of the difference in sounds is clearly seen. All other systems which do not agree with this are surely at fault. This is the measurement of the series of sound which correspond with nature.

I have stated before that to take SA-PA as $\frac{2}{3}$ and SA-MA as $\frac{3}{4}$ is only a rough calculation. Although this calculation is approximately correct when we proceed by the system we shall be never able to obtain the other Swarams namely $\frac{1}{2}$, $\frac{1}{3}$, $\frac{1}{4}$, $\frac{1}{5}$ and $\frac{1}{6}$.

Again, we have seen in one of the previous tables that when we proceed by SA-PA as $\frac{2}{3}$ the Sthayi does not end exactly but has 24 cents over, and 24 cents less when proceeding by SA-MA as $\frac{3}{4}$. Therefore it is quite clear that this system will never agree with that mentioned in ancient Isai-Tamil where the calculations are made by the trained ear of the musician. We consider that the calculation by geometrical progression is the one best suited to understand the system of the ancient Isai-Tamil.

We think that this system of the calculation of Srutis alone will satisfy the author of Tholkaupiam who speaks of the four different kinds of Yal — Marutham, Kurinji, Neythal and Palai,—Ilankavodigal, who mentions the four Jathis,—Ahanilai, Puranilai, Arugial and Perugial when change of Graham is made for each of the Yals, and Sarnga Dev who advocates change of Graham of Srutis. Any other system will not be so very minute as this.

We might have heard the gramaphone which records the sweet sounds of man and reproduces them. We also know that the reproduced voice does not altogether resemble the particular human voice. When we ask the why of it, we find that it is due to the fact that the recorder which receives the human sound is made of mica and thin plates of zinc, and that there is a vast difference between this and the recorder inside the human ear. In the same way the recording of sounds by the siren and that by the human ear will only be approximately the same and not completely so.

In the systems of Ayapalai and Vattapalai in use among the ancient Tamils, it is distinctly stated that the Sthayi comes to an end in the 12 Rasis by the SA-PA or the concordant series and SA-MA or branch series. It is this calculation for the 12 Swarams of the Sthayi that corresponds with that system. We have noted in the Tamil book p. 822 how the seven Swarams out of the 12 occur in the six mother Ragas with particular intervals. We have also stated in p. 823, the different Alakus for the six mother Ragas in the 12 Swarams. The Alakus for the 12 Swarams obtained by the SA-PA and the SA-MA series are given in p. 824 and 825 of the Tamil book.

These are the 12 Swarams used in Ayapalai pertaining to the 14 Kovais found in Senkotiyal. These are the Swarams used even by the apes which lived on the shores of Lemuria noted for its Isai-Tamil.

There was a good deal of controversy and doubt as regards these 12 Swarams and these came to an end only about 120 years ago in Europe. These were first used by Haydn (1732-1809) and Mozart (1756-1826). As the 12 Swarams of the octave were equally divided and pianos constructed, modulation in all the keys became possible. This modulation was brought to perfection by the celebrated Beethoven (1770-1827) about 120 years ago. So Equal Temperament was introduced as recently as 120 years ago. These are the 12 Swarams divided into equal semitones in Equal Temperament.

Captain Day mentions that before Equal Temperament was introduced into Europe, Indian musicians have used it in the music of the Yal. These are the 12 Swarams used by Mathavi 2000 years ago in the Sakota Yal with 2 Sthayis and 14 Kovais.

These are the 12 Swarams of the Vattapalai (where Oolai occurs as Kural) mentioned in the *Paripadal* of the poet Nallanduvanar who flourished at the close of the third Sangam about 3000 years ago. The Stanza is as follows:—

"பூவூது வண்டினம் யாழ்கொண்ட கொளை கேண்மின்
கொளைப்பொரு டேரிதரக் கொளுத்தாமற் குரல்கொண்ட
இன்னிசைத் தாங்கொளைச் சீர்க்குங்கிளைச்சுற்ற
வுழைச்சுரும்பின் கேழ்கெழு பாலையிசை யோர்மின்"

The four kinds of Yal, Marutham, Kurinji, Neythal, Palai, mentioned by the author of Tholkaupium who flourished at the close of the first Sangam about 8000 years ago, and the four kinds of Yal in Vattapalai derived from SA-MA and PA-NI are all derived from these 12 Swarams.

So we conclude from the above that even as early as 8000 years ago, and even at an earlier age from the commencement of the first Sangam i.e., 12000 years ago, the ancient Tamilians have had their Ganam with these 12 Swarams as the basis.

Some more beautiful points of coincidence which are found in the above calculations will be noticed in the calculation of Srutis that follows.

The 12 Swarams of the Ayapalai of the ancient Tamilians and the mathematical calculation of the Swarams compared with the calculations of other writers.

We have noticed till now what the measurements of the 12 Swarams of the Ayapalai were. The mathematical calculations of Srutis and Swarams by various writers were mentioned in Part II. We think it necessary to compare in this place their fractional lengths of wires and cents calculations with ours, especially in places where they most agree.

For, the measurement $\frac{2}{3}$ for Pa and $\frac{3}{4}$ for Ma has been used by many musicians of repute for many thousand years. We now take it upon ourselves to controvert their time-honoured theory by giving a new one which is in accordance with the systems of Ayapalai and Vattapalai in use among the Tamilians of South Madura for ages. Hence the necessity for the comparison.

The following table is divided into two sections. The first section shows how the Swarams proceed gradually upwards from Athara Sa or 1 to Madhya Sa or 2 in the order of 1, 2, 3, 4 &c. These are the Swarams that satisfy the rule of the ancient Tamilians and of musicians like Sarnga Dev and Bharata that Swarams should be a gradually ascending series which do not admit of any other possible Swaram in the middle. We do not think that there is any other correct method. Musicians of repute must acknowledge this.

If the logarithms found in Col. 4 be each of them multiplied by 1200 and divided by the logarithm of 2, we get the cents found in col. 5. These also are an ascending series like 1, 2, 3 with equal intervals. This is the opinion of the ancient Tamilians as well as that of Sarnga Dev. The mathematical calculations for the Sruti system of Sarnga Dev are seen in the Table in page 406.

Because of the difference owing to the necessity of accounting for the 22 Srutis in the octave there is an addition of 9 cents for each of the Swarams. Otherwise they will be correct. This will be seen in col. 10 of the Table in page 406.

In the second part the Swarasthanams which are in dispute at the present day, the fractions showing their respective lengths in the wire, their corresponding cents and their differences are given. They say that these measurements are those of the natural series and resemble the measurements which are determined by the siren. But we see the discrepencies in them in col. 8.

As these proceed with the presumption that Sa-Pa $=\frac{2}{3}$ and Sa-Ma $=\frac{3}{4}$ they have been driven to the necessity of selecting some from the Sa-Pa series, some from the Sa-Ma series and a few others from Sa-Ga series. As these have different measurements

The 12 Swarams of the Ayapalai of the ancient Tamilians and the mathematical calculation of the Swarams compared with the calculations of other writers.

The calculation of the 12 Swarams which are in Geometrical Progression with equal measurements.						The calculation of others who take SA-PA to be $\frac{2}{3}$ and SA-MA to be $\frac{3}{4}$.		
Number.	Rasi.	Names of Srutis and Alakus.	How the 12 Swarams proceed gradually upwards from 1 to 2, by powers of $\sqrt[12]{2}$	The logarithm of the powers of $\sqrt[12]{2}$	The cents of Ellis for the 12 Swarams	The fractional length of wire.	The cents corresponding to the fractions.	The intervals for the 12 Swarams.
1	2		3	4	5	6	7	8
0	Idapam	S	$(\sqrt[12]{2})^{0}$	·000000000	0			
1	Midunam	R_2	$(\sqrt[12]{2})^{1}$	·025085833	100	$\frac{15}{16}$	112	112
2	Kadagam	R_1	$(\sqrt[12]{2})^{2}$	·050171667	200	$\frac{8}{9}$	204	92
3	Simham	G_2	$(\sqrt[12]{2})^{3}$	·075257500	300	$\frac{5}{6}$	316	111
4	Kanni	G_1	$(\sqrt[12]{2})^{4}$	·100343333	400	$\frac{4}{5}$	386	71
5	Thulam	M_2	$(\sqrt[12]{2})^{5}$	·125429167	500	$\frac{3}{4}$	498	112
6	Viruchigam	M_1	$(\sqrt[12]{2})^{6}$	·150515000	600	$\frac{32}{45}$	590	92
7	Thanusu	P_2	$(\sqrt[12]{2})^{7}$	·175600833	700	$\frac{2}{3}$	702	112
8	Magaram	D_2	$(\sqrt[12]{2})^{8}$	·200686667	800	$\frac{5}{8}$	814	112
9	Kumbam	D_1	$(\sqrt[12]{2})^{9}$	·225772500	900	$\frac{3}{5}$	884	70
10	Meenam	N_2	$(\sqrt[12]{2})^{10}$	·250858333	1000	$\frac{9}{16}$	996	112
11	Mesham	N_1	$(\sqrt[12]{2})^{11}$	·275944167	1100	$\frac{8}{15}$	1088	92
12	Idapam	S_2	$(\sqrt[12]{2})^{12}$	·301030000	1200	$\frac{1}{2}$	1200	112

we see without any doubt that they cannot be used for singing Grahaswaram nor can they account for the six mother Ragas derived by the change of Grahaswaram. We have noted above how the 12 Swarams are obtained as a gradually ascending series in Vattapalai either as Sa-Pa or concordant Swarams or as Sa-Ma or branch Swarams without any other possible Swaram in the middle.

To sum up, then, we distinctly see that the Swarams and their measurements as given in Ayapalai by the ancients are the correct ones. The System of $\frac{2}{3}$ and $\frac{3}{4}$ of Pythagoras, and the theory of 22 Srutis of Sarnga Dev and Bharata are completely wrong and they are altogether unfit for purposes of Grahaswaram.

11. The mathematical calculations to prove that the 24 Srutis of the Vattapalai of the ancient Tamilians are the Srutis of the modern Karnatic music.

(Karunamirtha Sagaram in Tamil Page 840 and 844)

We have established now beyond doubt that the 12 Swarams obtained by the ancient Tamilians by the Sa-Pa and Sa-Ma systems are the Ayapalai, that these 12 are the very Swarams in use in modern Karnatic music, and that by rising gradually in geometrical progression they satisfy the principle that the series should be a gradually ascending one without admitting any other possible sound in the middle. Their number of vibrations has also been recorded. We should next proceed to find out how many of these Srutis occur between Athara Sa and Madhya Sa and give their mathematical calculation also.

In Part III we have divided a Sthayi into 12 Rasis, stating the concordant and discordant Swarams in each. We have also stated that two Swarams in particular Rasis should each of them be sung with one Alaku less and the Srutis then will be 24 in number when these 2 Alakus are added on.

Out of the 7 Swarams of an ascending and descending scale, the ancient Tamilians had made Ganam with 2 Alakus less either in two of the concordant or 2 of the branch Swarams.

From this it is clear that the ancients divided a Sthayi into 12 parts, and made 24 Srutis with 2 Alakus for each of the 12, and made their Ganam with 2 Alakus less in some cases, and not that they divided the octave itself into 22 Alakus. This theory of 22 Srutis seems to have been given out by mistake by Sarnga Dev, about 700 years ago when those who knew the rules and secrets of ancient music had become extinct.

We have mentioned here and there in many places that there can be but 24 Srutis in the octave and that any system which advocates either more or less can never satisfy the rules of Karnatic music which had always used 24 Srutis in its Ganams.

We have given a few Ragas as examples where even modern Karnatic music uses only 22 Srutis out of the 24 omitting two concordant and branch Srutis. The author of Sangeeta Ratnakaram speaks of the number of Srutis as 1, 2, 3, 4, 9, 22, 66 and even says there are numberless Srutis but finally settles it as 22. These 22 Srutis are nothing but the 22 out of the 24 Alakus of Isai-Tamil used by the Tamilians. Two Alakus have been reduced in Vilari and Kaikilai.

The mathematical calculations to show that the 24 Sru is of Vattapalai of the ancient Tamilians are the identical Srutis in use in modern Karnatic music.

Number.	Rasi.	Name of Sruti and Alagu.	How the 24 Srutis proceed upwards gradually from 1 to 2 by the powers of $\sqrt[24]{2}$	Logarithm of $\sqrt[24]{2}$	Anti-logarithms for logs given in col. 4	Number of vibrations of each Swaram if SA=540.	Number of vibrations of each Swaram if SA=240.	Location of the 24 Swarams in the first half of the total length of wire.	Location of the 24 Swarams in a wire 32 inches long.	Measurement by inches of each Swaram while proceeding from Athara SA.	The intervas between Swarams.	Cents for the 24 Swarams.
1		2	3	4	5	6	7	8	9	10	11	12
		S_2	$\sqrt[24]{2}$	·000000000	1·0000	540·0000	240·00	1·0000000	32·00000			0
1	Midunam	R_1	,, t^1	·012542917	1·0293	555·8232	247·03	0·9715320	31·08902	·9110	·9110	50
2		R_2	,, t^2	·025085833	1·0595	572·1103	254·28	0·9438743	30·20398	1·7960	·8850	100
3	Kadagam	R_3	,, t^3	·037628750	1·0905	588·8743	261·72	0·9170042	29·34413	2·6559	·8599	150
4		R_4	,, t^4	·050171667	1·1225	606·1295	269·40	0·8908986	28·50876	3·4913	·8354	200
5	Simmum	G_1	,, t^5	·062714583	1·1554	623·8905	277·30	0·8655366	27·69717	4·3028	·8115	250
6		G_2	,, t^6	·075257500	1·1892	642·1719	285·41	0·8408964	26·90868	5·0913	·7885	300
7	Kanni	G_3	,, t^7	·087800417	1·2241	660·9890	293·78	0·8169577	26·14265	5·8574	·7661	350
8		G_4	,, t^8	·100343333	1·2599	680·3574	302·38	0·7937005	25·39842	6·6016	·7442	400
9	Thulam	M_1	,, t^9	·112886250	1·2968	700·2934	311·23	0·7711055	24·67538	7·3246	·7230	450
10		M_2	,, t^{10}	·125429167	1·3348	720·8136	320·36	0·7491535	23·97291	8·0271	.7025	500
11	Viruchigam	M_3	,, t^{11}	·137972083	1·3740	741·9350	329·76	0·7278265	23·29045	8·7096	·6826	550
12		M_4	,, t^{12}	·150515000	1·4142	763·6754	339·41	0·7071069	22·62742	9·3726	·6630	600
											·6441	

The mathematical calculations to show that the 24 Srutis of Vattapalai of the ancient Tamilians are the identical Srutis in use in modern Karnatic music.

Number.	Rasi.	Name of Sruti and Alagu.	How the 24 Srutis proceed upwards gradually from 1 to 2 by the powers of $\sqrt[24]{2}$	Logarithm of $\sqrt[24]{2}$	Anti-logarithms for logs given in col-4	Number of vibrations of each Swaram if SA=540.	Number of vibrations of each Swaram if SA=240.	Location of the 24 Swarams in the first half of the total length of wire	Location of the 24 Swarams in a wire 32 inches long.	Measurement by inches of each Swaram while proceeding from Athara SA.	The intervals between Swarams.	Cents for the 24 Swarams.
1		2	3	4	5	6	7	8	9	10	11	12
13	Thanusu	P_1	$\sqrt[24]{2}$ t13	.163057917	1·4557	786·0528	349·37	0·6869768	21·98326	10·0167		650
14		P_2	,, t14	.175600833	1·4983	809·0858	359·50	0·6674199	21·35744	10·6426	·6259	700
15	Magaram	D_1	,, t15	·188143750	1·5422	832·7939	370·13	0·6484198	20·74944	11·2506	·6080	750
16		D_2	,, t16	·200686667	1·5874	857·1966	380·98	0·6299601	20·15872	11·8413	·5907	800
17	Kumbam	D_3	,, t17	.213229583	1·6340	882·3145	392·16	0·6120268	19·58486	12·4151	·5738	850
18		D_4	,, t18	·225772500	1·6818	908·1681	403·63	0·5946036	19·02732	12·9727	·5576	900
19	Meenam	N_1	,, t19	·238315417	1·7311	934·7794	415·46	0·5776764	18·48564	13·5144	·5317	950
20		N_2	,, t20	·250858333	1·7818	962·1707	427·63	0·5612810	17·95939	14·0406	·5262	1000
21	Medam	N_3	,, t21	·263401250	1·8440	990·3644	440·16	0·5452539	17·44812	14·5519	·5113	1050
22		N_4	,, t22	·275944167	1·8877	1019·3844	453·05	0·5297315	16·95141	15·0489	·4967	1100
23	Idabam	S_1	,, t23	·288487083	1·9431	1049·2546	466·34	0.51465110	16·46883	15·5312	·4826	1150
24		S_2	,, t24	·301030000	2·0000	1080·0000	480.00	0.5000000	16·00000	16·0000	·4688	1200

We emphatically say that Sarnga Dev is wrong when he says that there are 22 Srutis in the octave and that if the octave be so divided the resultant Swarams and Srutis will never satisfy Karnatic music.

We, again, emphatically assert that the ancient Tamilians about 12000 years ago used the 7 Swarams of the Sthayi, the 12 half Swarams of a Rasi Vattam, and the 24 Alakus of Srutis which have 2 Alakus in each of the 12 Rasis, as Ayapalai and Vattapalai of Isai-Tamil. Their system of Vattapalai clearly indicates that the Srutis of Karnatic music are 24 and that they never mentioned 22 Srutis in the octave.

Just as we gave before the mathematical calculations and measurements of the 12 Swarams, we must now determine the measurements of the 24 Srutis in the octave.

Granting that, according to the theory of the ancients, if Athara SA be 1 Madhya SA is 2, the 24 Alakus or Swarams should be produced here just as the 12 Swarams generated from Ayapalai as a gradually ascending series with no other possible Swarams between.

12. Mathematical calculation to show the minute Srutis that are in use in the South Indian or Karnatic music.

(Karunamirtha Sagaram in Tamil Page 849—859.)

To those scholars who are anxious to know the antiquity and minuteness of South Indian music we are sure what we have stated hitherto is quite enough to convince them. It is a matter for great wonder that such rare things have been mentioned many thousands of years ago, and that they throw into shade the advanced opinions of the modern day. However we must not stop here but consider another thing of very great importance. The sweet Ragas we are in the habit of singing are not confined to the seven Swarams or the 12 half Swarams or even the 24 Swarams. Unless we have a definite knowledge of this, our doubts will be often recurring.

If we notice the Swarams used in the 10000 ancient Isais found in works on Isai-Tamil in use in the ancient Tamil country or the Swarams used in the *Puns* like Thirugnanam, Thevaram and Thiruvachakam according to the ancient system, we shall be surprised to find that more Srutis than 24, and minuter ones, are found in them. The *Puns* and Ragas of ancient times have had their names changed and sung at the modern day as Parsi. Hindustani and English notes to suit modern tastes. Very seldom we come across the beautiful chanting of the ancient Thevara *Puns* and the rare excellence which they had in convincing the minds of the hearers. Next to them in beauty come the Kshetrya *Pathams*. Even these, we find, have become rare.

The beauty of old Ragas should be attributed to the minute Srutis in which they were sung. As it was difficult to determine what those Srutis were, even the seven primary Swarams were doubted. When one of these minute Swarams occurred along with the seven Swarams, it was found to be a little higher or lower in pitch. So this made them say "there is a difference between your Swarams and ours, your Swarams are incorrect." They not only argued this way but tried to produce different measurements in support of their statement. But this only increased the confusion still more, and no definiteness was arrived at.

So long as we do not understand these minute Srutis, the minuteness of ancient Isai-Tamil will be a sealed book to us, nor could we understand the subtlety of modern Ragas which are sung according to ancient rules. We could not write out the Swarams and Srutis for the modern Ragas either. The result will be that the minuteness of the musical system will gradually disappear and we shall have to rest content with 12 Swarams only. Others might also accuse us of singing Karnatic Ragas incorrectly, without knowing the Srutis. Just as the Karnatic Ragas have lost their ancient Tamil names and are called by foreign names, so they might, in course of time, lose their minute Swarams also and be reduced to music with 12 Swarams only. So we see the necessity of studying these minute Srutis deeply.

1. We have noted before that the 12 Swarams obtained by the SA-PA and SA-MA principle, or the concordant and branch Swarams of Vattapalai in the 12 Rasis, are the 12 Swarams of Ayapalai. Of these seven Swarams, each of the Swarams RI, GA, MA, DHA and NI with the exception of Kural and Ili (SA and PA) is divided into two and thus (10+2) the 12 Swarams are obtained.

2. The 12 half Swarams of Vattapalai have 2 Alakus each, thus accounting for the 24 Srutis or Alakus of Vattapalai.

3. We see from experience that the 24 Alakus of Vattapalai had each of them 2 Sub-Alakus and were used in South Indian music.

4. Further, these 48 Sruti Sthanams are still subdivided into halves and the resultant 96 Srutis are profusely used in our Karnatic music.

To sum up, then, we have reason to think that Ayapalai is the division of the seven Swarams into the twelve.

The 12 Swarams of Ayapalai when divided into 24 Srutis become Vattapalai.

The 24 Srutis of Vattapalai when sub-divided into 48 Srutis or Alakus become Thirikonapalai.

And the 48 Srutis of Alakus of Thirikonapalai when halved into 96 quarter Srutis become Chathurapalai.

For, mention is made of four Palais, Ayapalai, Vattapalai, Thirikonapali, and Chathurapalai. We see from their calculations that just as they used half Swarams in Ayapalai they have used quarter Swarams in Vattapalai. So the third and fourth sub-divisions naturally formed the Thirikonapalai and Chathurapalai. There is evidence, then, to conclude that

the 12 half-Swarams are Ayapalai
the 24 quarter Swarams are Vattapalai
the 48 one eight Swarams are Thirikonapalai
the 96 one-sixteenth Swarams are Chathurapalai

(1) They have said that there are 12 Palais, 7 primary and 5 secondary, in the system of Ayapalai, and have derived the six mother Ragas.–Chempalai, Padumalaipalai,

Chevvalipali, Arumpalai Kodipalai and Vilaripalai corresponding to the modern Sankara-paranam, Karaharapiria, Hanumathodi, Kalyani, Harikambodi and Natabhairavi, from them and also the four branch Ragas or Janiya Ragas, viz Pun, Punniam, Thiram, Thiratthiram corresponding to Sampooranam, Shadavam, Oudavam and Suvarantham.

(2) They have also stated clearly the four primary Puns derived from Vatta-palai, namely, Marutham, Kurinji, Neythal and Palai, the four Jathis derived from each of them, namely Ahanilai, Puranilai, Arugial, and Perugial, as well as the system of making ganam with one Alaku less in Vilari and Kaikilai. There is reason to think that Ilankovadigal might have omitted the details of Thirikonapalai and Chathurapalai as he had explicitly stated the first two very minutely.

We can never clear our doubts if we take the standard of $\frac{2}{3}$ and $\frac{3}{4}$ which never completely finish an octave. We can never make ganam with only 22 Srutis in the octave. If we admit the 22 Srutis for the octave some of the Srutis used in South Indian music will never be found there. It will be more to the point if the Sthayi were divided into 12 parts, and if one or more of $\frac{1}{96}$ Srutis be added along with the seven main Swarams. Therefore it is necessary to give those mathematical calculations and practically demonstrate the fact by means of the Ragas in which those very minute Swarams occur.

We need not dilate upon these mathematical calculations as they are the same given before for the 12 Swarams and the 24 Srutis.

" மூலாதாரந் தொடங்கிய மூச்சைக் காலாற்கிளப்பிக் கருத்தாலியக்கி ஒன்றெனத்தாக்கி இரண்டெனப் பகுத்துப் பண்ணீர்மைகளைப் பிறப்பிக்கப்பட்ட மிடற்றுப்பாடலும் "

According to the above ancient Sootram which means that the breath which generates from the *Moolatharam*, proceeds upwards, is held in the mind, becomes a musical sound which increases in pitch from 1 to 2; Puns are derived from this music which proceeds from the throat. We must see how between 1 or Athara Sa and 2 or Madhya Sa there are 96 equal divisions and 96 minute Srutis which form a gradually ascending series without admitting of any other possible Sruti between. As we have noticed before, if we divide the logarithm of 2 by 96 and multiply the result by the series 1, 2, 3, 4 up to 96 we get the figures in col. 4. The decimal fractions for the logarithms are found in col. 5; the vibrations, in col. 6 and 7; the parts of the length of the wire, in col. 8; the measurement of the wire in col. 9; the measurements of the respective Srutis, in col. 10; and the cents for each of the Srutis in cols. 11 and 12. All the above are clearly stated in the Table in the next page

The mathematical calculations for the 12 Swarams of the **Ayapalai** known among the ancient Tamilians, the 24 Srutis of the Vattapalai and **the 96** minute Srutis.

Number.	Rasi.	How the 96 Srutis are a gradually ascending series from 1 to 2 shown by the powers of $\sqrt[96]{2}$		The logarithms of the powers $\sqrt[96]{2}$	Anti-logarithms for the figures given in col. 4	Number of vibrations of each Swaram if SA=540.	Number of vibrations of each Swaram if SA=240.	Location of the 96 Swarams in the first half of the total length of wire	Location of the 96 Swarams in the first half of a wire 32 inches long.	Measurement by inches of each Swaram while proceeding from Atharа SA.	Cents for the 96 Swarams.	The intervals between the Swarams.
1	Swaram.	2	3 Sruti.	4	5	6	7	8	9	10	11	12
		$\sqrt[96]{2}$		.000000000	1·0000	540·00	240·00	1·000000	32·000000	·0000	·0	
1	1 Midunam Ri	,, t^1		·003135729	1·0072	543·89	241·73	0·992805	31·769760	·2302	12·5	12·5
2		,, t^2		·006271458	1·0145	547·83	243·48	0·985663	31·541216	·4588	25·0	12·5
3		,, t^3		·009407187	1·0219	551·83	245·26	0·978572	31·314304	·6857	37·5	12·5
4		,, t^4	1	·012542917	1·0293	555·84	247·03	0.971532	31·089024	·9110	50·0	12·5
5		,, t^5		·015678646	1.0368	559·87	248·83	0·964542	30·865360	1·1346	62·5	12.5
6		,, t^6		·018814375	1·0443	563·92	250·63	0·957603	30·643296	1·3567	75·0	12·5
7		,, t^7		.021950104	1·0518	567·97	252·43	0·950714	30·422848	1·5772	87·5	12·5
8		,, t^8	2	·025085833	1·0595	572·13	254·28	0·943874	30·203968	1·7960	100·0	12·5
9	2 Kadagam Ri	,, t^9		·028221563	1·0671	576·30	256·10	0·937084	29·986688	2·0133	112·5	12·5
10		,, t^{10}		·031357292	1·0749	580·48	257·98	0·930342	29·770944	2·2291	125.0	12·5
11		,, t^{11}		·034493021	1·0827	584·67	259·85	0·923649	29·556768	2·4432	137.5	12·5
12		,, t^{12}	3	.037628750	1·0905	588·87	261·72	0·917004	29·344128	2·6559	150.0	12·5
13		,, t^{13}		.040764479	1·0984	593·14	263·62	0·910407	29·133024	2·8670	162·5	12·5
14		,, t^{14}		.043900208	1·1064	597·46	275·54	0·903857	28·923424	3·0766	175·0	12·5
15		,, t^{15}		·047035938	1·1144	601·78	267·46	0·897355	28.715360	3·2846	187·5	12.5
16		,, t^{16}	4	·050171667	1·1225	606·15	269·40	0·890899	28·508755	3·4913	200·0	12 5

1		2	3	4	5	6	7	8	9	10	11	12
17	3 Simmum GA Swaram.	$\sqrt[96]{2}t^{17}$	Sruti.	·053307396	1·1306	610·52	271·34	0·884490	28·303664	3·6963	212·5	12·5
18		,, t^{18}		·056443125	1·1388	614·95	273·31	0·878126	28·100032	3·9000	225·0	12.5
19		,, t^{19}		·059578854	1·1470	619·38	275·28	0·871809	27·897872	4·1021	237·5	12·5
20		,, t^{20}	5	·062714583	1·1554	623·91	277·30	0·865537	27·697170	4·3028	250·0	12·5
21		,, t^{21}		·065850313	1·1638	628·45	279·31	0·859310	27.497910	4·5021	262·5	12·5
22		,, t^{22}		·068986042	1·1722	632·99	281·33	0·853118	27·299760	4·7002	275·0	12.5
23		,, t^{23}		·072121771	1·1807	637·58	283·37	0·846990	27·103688	4·8963	287·5	12·5
24		,, t^{24}	6	·075257500	1·1892	642·17	285·41	0·840896	26·908650	5·0913	300·0	12·5
25	4 Kanni GA	,, t^{25}		·078393229	1·1978	646·82	287·47	0·834847	26·715104	5·2849	312·5	12·5
26		,, t^{26}		·081528758	1·2065	651·51	289·56	0.828841	26·522912	5·4771	325·0	12·5
27		,, t^{27}		·084664688	1·2152	656·21	291·65	0·822878	26·332096	5·6679	337·5	12·5
28		,, t^{28}	7	·087800417	1·2241	660·97	293·78	0·816958	26·142646	5·8574	350·0	12·5
29		,, t^{29}		·090936146	1·2329	665·77	295·90	0·811080	25·954560	6·0455	362·5	12·5
30		,, t^{30}		·094071875	1·2419	670·63	298·06	0·805245	25·767840	6·2322	375·0	12·5
31		,, t^{31}		·097207604	1·2509	675·49	300·22	0·799452	25·582464	6·4175	387·5	12·5
32		,, t^{32}	8	·100343333	1·2599	680·35	302·38	0·793701	25·398416	6·6016	400·0	12·5
33	5 Thulam MA	,, t^{33}		·103479063	1·2691	685·31	304·58	0·787990	25·215680	6·7843	412·5	12·5
34		,, t^{34}		·106614792	1·2783	690·28	306·79	0·782322	25·034288	6·9657	425·0	12·5
35		,, t^{35}		·109750521	1·2875	695·25	309·00	0·776693	24·854176	7·1458	437·5	12·5
36		,, t^{36}	9	·112886260	1·2968	700·27	311·23	0·771106	24·675376	7·3246	450·0	12·5
37		,, t^{37}		·116021979	1·3062	705·35	313·49	0·765558	24·497843	7·5022	462·5	12·5
38		,, t^{38}		·119157708	1·3157	710·45	315·77	0·760050	24·321600	7·6784	475·0	12·5
39		,, t^{39}		·122293438	1·3252	715·60	318·05	0·754582	24·146624	7·8534	487·5	12·5
40		,, t^{40}	10	.125429167	1·3348	720·80	320·36	0·749154	23·972912	8·0271	500·0	12·5
41	6 Viruchigam MA	,, t^{41}		·128564896	1·3445	726·04	322·68	0·743764	23·800448	8·1996	512·5	12·5
42		,, t^{42}		.131700625	1·3543	731·32	325·03	0·738413	23·629216	8·3708	525·0	12.5
43		,, t^{43}		·134836354	1·3641	736·61	327·38	0·733100	23·459200	8·5408	537·5	12·5
44		,, t^{44}	11	·137972083	1·3740	741·96	329·76	0·727827	23·290448	8·7096	550·0	12.5
45		,, t^{45}		·141107813	1·3839	747·31	332·14	0·722591	23·122896	8·8871	562·5	12·5
46		,, t^{46}		·144243542	1·3939	752·71	334·54	0·717392	22·956544	9·0435	575·0	12·5
47		,, t^{47}		·147379271	1·4040	758·16	336·96	0·712231	22·791392	9·2086	587·5	12·5
48		,, t^{48}	12	·150515000	1·4142	763·67	339·41	0·707107	22·627421	9·3726	600·0	12·5

The mathematical calculations for the 12 Swarams of the Ayapalai known among the ancient Tamilians, the 24 Srutis of the Vattapalai and the 96 minute Srutis.

Number.	Rasi. How the 96 Srutis are a gradually ascending series from 1 to 2 shown by the powers of $\sqrt[96]{2}$	Sruti.	The Logarithms of the powers $\sqrt[96]{2}$	Anti-logarithms for the figures given in col. 4.	Number of vibrations of each Swaram if SA=540.	Number of vibrations of each Swaram if SA=240.	Location of the 96 Swarams in the first half of the total length of wire	Location of the 96 Swarams in the first half of a wire 32 inches long.	Measurement by inches of each Swaram while proceeding from Athara SA.	Cents for the 96 Swarams.	The intervals between the Swarams.
1	2	3	4	5	6	7	8	9	10	11	12
	7 Thanusu PA Swaram.										
49	$\sqrt[96]{2^{49}}$		·153650729	1·4245	769·23	341·88	0·702020	22·464644	9·5354	612·5	12·5
50	,, 2^{50}		·156786458	1·4348	774·79	344·35	0·696969	22·303008	9·6970	625·0	12·5
51	,, 2^{51}		·159922188	1·4452	780·41	346·85	0·691955	22·142560	9·8574	637·5	12·5
52	,, 2^{52}	13	·163057917	1·4557	786·08	349·37	0·686977	21·983258	10·0167	650·0	12·5
53	,, 2^{53}		·166193646	1·4662	791·75	351·89	0·682035	21·825104	10·1749	662·5	12·5
54	,, 2^{54}		·169329375	1·4768	797·47	354·43	0·677132	21·668234	10·3318	675·0	12·5
55	,, 2^{55}		·172465104	1·4875	803·25	357·00	0·672256	21·512205	10·4878	687·5	12·5
56	,, 2^{56}	14	·175600833	1·4983	809·08	359·50	0·667420	21·357440	10·6426	700·0	12·5
	8 Magaram DHA										
57	,, 2^{57}		·178736563	1·5092	814·96	362·21	0·662618	21·203776	10·7962	712·5	12·5
58	,, 2^{58}		·181872292	1·5201	820.85	364·82	0·657851	21·051232	10·9488	725·0	12·5
59	,, 2^{59}		·185008021	1·5311	826·79	367·47	0·653119	20·899792	11·1002	737·5	12.5
60	,, 2^{60}	15	·188143750	1·5422	832·79	370·13	0·648420	20·749440	11·2506	750·0	12·5
61	,, 2^{61}		·191279479	1·5534	838·83	372·82	0·643755	20·600160	11·3998	762·5	12·5
62	,, 2^{62}		·194415208	1·5646	844·88	375·50	0·639124	20·451952	11·5480	775·0	12·5
63	,, 2^{63}		·197550938	1·5760	851·04	378·24	0·634526	20·304816	11·6952	787·5	12·5
64	,, 2^{64}	16	·200686667	1·5874	857·20	380·98	0·629960	20·158723	11·8413	800·0	12·5

1		2	3	4	5	6	7	8	9	10	11	12
65	9 Kumbam Dʜᴀ Swaram.	$\sqrt{2}t^{65}$	Sruti.	·203822396	1·5989	863·41	383·74	0·625429	20·013715	11·9863	812·5	12·5
66		,, t^{66}		·206958125	1·6105	869·67	386·52	0·620929	19·869728	12·1303	825·0	12·5
67		,, t^{67}		·210093854	1·6222	875·99	389·33	0·616462	19·726984	12·2730	837·5	12·5
68		,, t^{68}	17	·213229583	1·6340	882·36	392·16	0·612027	19·584858	12·4151	850·0	12·5
69		,, t^{69}		·216365313	1·6458	888·73	394·99	0·607624	19·443952	12·5560	862·5	12·5
70		,, t^{70}		·219501042	1·6577	895·16	397·85	0·603252	19·304074	12·6959	875·0	12·5
71		,, t^{71}		·222636771	1·6697	901·64	400·73	0·598912	19·165184	12·8348	887·5	12·5
72		,, t^{72}	18	·225772500	1·6818	908·17	403·63	0·594604	19·027315	12·9727	900·0	12·5
73	10 Meenam Nɪ.	,, t^{73}		·228908229	1·6940	914·76	406·56	0·590326	18·890432	13·1096	912·5	12·5
74		,, t^{74}		·232043958	1·7062	921·35	409·49	0·586079	18·754528	13·2455	925·0	12·5
75		,, t^{75}		·235179688	1·7186	928·04	412·46	0·581863	18.619600	13·3804	937·5	12·5
76		,, t^{76}	19	·238315417	1·7311	934·79	415·46	0·577676	18·485645	13·5144	950·0	12·5
77		,, t^{77}		·241451146	1·7436	941·54	418·46	0·573520	18·352640	13·6474	962·5	12·5
78		,, t^{78}		·244586875	1·7563	948·40	421·51	0·569394	18·220608	13·7794	975·0	12·5
79		,, t^{79}		·247722604	1·7690	955·26	424·56	0·565298	18·089536	13·9105	987·5	12·5
80		,, t^{80}	20	·250858333	1·7819	962·17	427·63	0·561231	17·959392	14·0406	1000·0	12·5
81	11 Medam Nɪ	,, t^{81}		·253994063	1·7947	969·14	430·73	0·557198	17·830189	14·1698	1012·5	12·5
82		,, t^{82}		·257129792	1·8077	976·16	433·85	0·553185	17·701904	14·2981	1025·0	12·5
83		,, t^{83}		·260265521	1·8208	983·23	436·99	0·549205	17·574560	14·4254	1037·5	12·5
84		,, t^{84}	21	·263401250	1·8440	990·36	440·16	0·545254	17·448125	14·5519	1050·0	12·5
85		,, t^{85}		·266536979	1·8473	997·54	443·35	0·541331	17·322592	14·6774	1062·5	12·5
86		,, t^{86}		·269672708	1·8607	1008·74	446·57	0·537437	17·197968	14·8020	1075·0	12·5
87		,, t^{87}		·272808438	1·8742	1012·07	449·81	0.533570	17·074240	14·9258	1087·5	12·5
88		,, t^{88}	22	·275944167	1·8877	1019·36	453·05	0·529732	16·951408	15·0486	1100·0	12·5
89	12 Idabam Sᴀ	,, t^{89}		279079896	1·9014	1026·76	456·34	0·525920	16·829440	15·1706	1112·5	12·5
90		,, t^{90}		·282215625	1·9152	1034·21	459·65	0·522137	16·708384	15·2916	1125·0	12·5
91		,, t^{91}		·285351354	1·9291	1041·71	462·98	0·518380	16·588160	15·4118	1137·5	12·5
92		,, t^{92}	23	·288487083	1·9431	1049·27	466·34	0·514651	16·468835	15·5312	1150·0	12·5
93		,, t^{93}		·291622813	1·9571	1056·83	469·70	0·510949	16·350352	15·6496	1162·5	12·5
94		,, t^{94}		·294758542	1·9713	1064·50	473·11	0·507273	16·232726	15·7673	1175·0	12·5
95		,, t^{95}		·297894271	1·9856	1072·22	476·54	0·503623	16·115936	15·8841	1187·5	12·5
96		,, t^{96}	24	·301030000	2·0000	1080·00	480·00	0·500000	16·000000	16·0000	1200·0	12·5

The four minute Srutis for each of the major Srutis are separately shown in the Table

Each Rasi is divided into 2 Alakus and each Alaku into 4 Srutis.

When any of the above Srutis is to be sounded, the modern method is to sound it as a Gamakam by pulling the string towards the player from one of the twelve frets. We must first determine exactly the resemblance between the Sruti played as a Gamakam and that sounded by the human voice and try to reproduce it in the Veena by the help of small frets. We may thus arrive at the minute Srutis ¼, ½ and ¾. Again, the 12 Sthanams of the Table, namely like 8, 16, 24, 32, 40 &c. are the 12 half Swarams of the Ayapalai. And the Sthanams like 4, 8, 12, 16, 20, 24 &c. are the 24 quarter Swarams of the Vattapalai. The others are more minute Srutis which are the ¼, ½ or the ¾ of any particular Sruti.

These indicate the Srutis of the Vattapalai known to the ancient Tamilians in the 12 Rasis. These are shown separately and distinctly. so that the 24 Srutis obtained by dividing each Rasi into 2 Alakus, and the more minute Srutis obtained by sub-dividing each Alaku into 4, might be clearly understood.

Each of the Swarams here will stand to the other either in the relation of concordant or branch Swaram. In the same way among these concordant and branch Swarams, any Alaku which comes as Gamakam and its four minute Srutis will be in the same harmonious relation

For example, the Ri with 4 Alakus ending in Kadakam (line 16) will have the Sa-Pa or concordant relation with Dha which ends in Kumbam. In the same way when this Ri is used as Gamakam by adding the 2 Srutis in the 18th Sthanam, the Dha also in Kumbam will be used as Gamakam by taking in the 2 Srutis in line 74. These are the Ri and the Dha used in Sankaraparanam.. They must be stated as Ri and Dha with 4½ Alakus each.

Again, the Ri with 4½ Alakus occurring in Arabi derived from Deera Sankaraparanam (line 17) and the Dha with 4¼ Alakus (in line 73) are concordant Srutis. Examples of the same kind of minute Srutis may be seen in the Tables that follow.

When these concordant and branch Swarams are mentioned in the 12 Rasis, they become Gamakams either as ¼, ½, ¾, 1, 1¼, 1½ or 1¾ Srutis obtaining the names of the Swarams which stand in the respective Rasis. For instance the Ri which ends with four Alakus in Kadagam obtains 4¼, 4½, 4¾, 5, 5¼, 5½, 5¾ Alakus in the 17th, 18th, 19th, 20th, 21st and 23 places (with the exception of the 24th place) while occurring in Simham, and is used as Gamakam.

Again, the Ri with 2 Alakus which finishes at the 8th place in Mithunam occurs in thr 16th Sthanam in Kadagam with 2¼, 2½, 2¾, 3, 3¼, 3½ and 3¾ Alakus (omitting Ri with 4 Alakus) corresponding to the places 9, 10, 11, 12, 13, 14 and 15. These may be clearly seen in the Tables that follow.

We presume our readers do now clearly understand the mathematical calculations for the 12 half Swarams of Ayapalai, the 24 quarter Srutis of Vattapalai, the 48 one-eighth Srutis of Thirikonapalai and the 96 one sixteenth Srutis of Chathurapalai. Though we come across many varied names for the Swarams, the Srutis of South Indian music have been made clear by works on Isai-Tamil and Telugu literature. Therefore, it is clear that the modern names do correspond with those given in ancient Tamil works, and the Sanskrit names derived from the ancient Tamil names may also be used.

13. Names of Swarams and Srutis.

What we now call Suddha Ri and Chathursruti Ri, and Suddha Dha and Chathursruti Dha are only the Swarams of Ayapalai with 2 Alakus and 4 Alakus. What the ancient Tamilians called Alaķus, modern writers name Srutis. The Swarams Ri, Ga, Ma, Dha and Ni with two Srutis each are now called by us Suddha Ri, Suddha Ga, Suddha Ma, Suddha Dha, and Suddha Ni. In the same manner the Swarms Ri, Ga, Ma, Dha, and Ni with 4 Alakus each are known at the present day as Chathursruti Ri, Chathursruti Dha, Sadarana Ga, Prathi Ma and Kaisika Ni.

The Swarams in the Table that follows appear to have names in correspondence with the Alakus in the 12 Rasis.

But it is within our experience that we see Ga in the house belonging to Ri, and *vice versa*, and Dha in that of Ni and *vice versa*. This is also seen in the 12 Palais obtained by the 12 Swarams of the Rasis by taking each of the Rasis as the compartment of Sa in order. It may be seen in line 4 of the Table of change of Graham on page 720 of my Tamil Book that in the fourth secondary Palai Ga occurs in the compartment of Ri with 4 Alakus, and Ni in the compartment of Dha with 4 Alakus. In the same way in line 9 Ni occurs in the compartment of Dha$_1$, and in line 11, Ga in that of Ri$_1$ and Ni in that of Dha$_1$. In other words Ni gives up its two compartments and comes as far as one of the compartments of Ri. So we find here that Ga and Ni occur in three Rasis with six Alakus. In the same way when Ri gives up its second compartment and takes the third which belongs to Ga, it obtains six Alakus in all the three Rasis. These Ri and Dha with six Alakus we call Shat Sruti. To bring out the same meaning the Ga with six Srutis is called by us Andara Gandharam or end Gandharam and the second Ni as Kakali or sweet Ni. All these details may be seen in the Table that follows.

In addition to this, we should find the names for the 24 Alakus of Vattapalai and the Vikruti Swarams derived from them.

In the Table that follows we may see the modern names as well as the names that were used without any doubt in ancient times.

The names of 24 Alakus of Vattapalai with the modern names of Srutis and their position.

Number.	The names used at present and the names that ought to be used.					The names of Srutis according to the system of Vattapalai.
1	...		S		Nethasadjam or Achutha-sadjam ...	Sa or ... ... Kural
2	Ega Sruti Rishabam ...	1	R			1 Alaku Ri Thuttham
3	Suddha Rishabam ...	2	R			2 Alaku Ri ... ,,
4	Tis Sruti Rishabam ...	3	R	G	1 Ega Sruti Gandharam ...	3 Alaku Ri or 1 Alaku Ga Kaikilai ... ...
5	Chatur Sruti Rishabam ...	4	R	G	2 Suddha Gandharam ...	4 Alaku Ri or 2 Alaku Ga Kaikilai ... ...
6	Pancha Sruti Rishabam ...	5	R	G	3 Tis Sruti Gandharam ...	5 Alaku Ri or 3 Alaku Ga Kaikilai ... ...
7	Shat Sruti Rishabam ...	6	R	G	4 Sadarana Gandharam ...	6 Alaku Ri or 4 Alaku Ga Kaikilai ... ...
8	Sutha Gandara Rishabam	7	R	G	5 Pancha Sruti Gandharam.	7 Alaku Ri or 5 Alaku Ga Kaikilai ... ...
9	...			G	6 Andhara Gandharam ...	6 Alaku Ga Kaikilai
10	Sutha Madhimum ...	1	M	G	7 Sutha Madhima Gandharam	7 Alaku Ga or 1 Alaku Ma Oolai ... ...
11	Suddha Madhimum ...	2	M			2 Alaku Ma ... Oolai
12	Tis Sruthi Madhimum ...	3	M			3 Alaku Ma ... ,,
13	Prathi Madhimum ...	4	M			4 Alaku Ma ... ,,
14	Sutha Panchama Madhimum	5	M	P	Sutha Panchamum ...	5 Alaku Ma or 1 Alaku Pa Oolai ... ...
15	...		P	P	Panchamum or Achutha-panchamum ...	Pa or ... Ili
16	Ega Sruti Dhaivatham ...	1	D			1 Alaku Dha
17	Suddha Dhaivatham ...	2	D			2 Alaku Dha ... Vilari
18	Tis Sruti Dhaivatham ...	3	D	N	1 Ega Sruti Nishadam ...	3 Alaku Dha or 1 Alaku Ni Tharam ... ...
19	Chatur Sruti Dhaivatham ...	4	D	N	2 Suddha Nishadam ...	4 Alaku Dha or 2 Alaku Ni Tharam ... ...
20	Pancha Sruti Dhaivatham	5	D	N	3 Tis Sruti Nishadam ...	5 Alaku Dha or 3 Alaku Ni Tharam ... ...
21	Shat Sruthi Dhaivatham ...	6	D	N	4 Kaisika Nishadam ...	6 Alaku Dha or 4 Alaku Ni Tharam ... ...
22	Sutha Nishada Dhaivatham	7	D	N	5 Pancha Sruti Nishadam ...	7 Alaku Dha or 5 Alaku Ni Tharam ... ...
23	...			N	6 Kakali Nishadam ...	6 Alaku Ni ...Tharam
24	Sutha Shadjam ...		S	N	7 Sutha Shadja Nishadam ...	7 Alaku Ni or 1 Alaku Sa
25	Shadjam ...		S		Natha or Achutha Shadjam	Sa

Of these, the names of the 12 Swarams with 2 Alakus each are the same as given in the previous Table. We know that it is quite possible to have a third Alaku between the second and the fourth and a fifth between the fourth and the sixth Alakus. On the same principle I have marked a Dwisruti RI between Suddha RI and Chathursruti RI and a Pancha Sruti RI between Chathursruti RI and Shatsruti RI. It is clearly seen that Sutha SA and Sutha PA have each a Sruti less than SA and PA, and that Achyuta SA and Achyuta PA are Niyata Srutis. Of these, Niyata (நியத) SA and PA, being the very fundamental Srutis of all music, can admit of no change. But the NI below SA and the MA below PA are called Sutha Shadja NI and Sutha Pancha MA respectively. From this it does not follow that we should make Ganam with the 2 Srutis of SA and the 2 Srutis of PA left out. On the other hand, the Ragas should be made after changing the Graham according to the system of Ayapalai, and Ganam should be made with a few Alakus less according to the system of Vattapalai. Perhaps we may hesitate a little and say that if we change the Graham in accordance with the four Srutis of SA and PA we should obtain innumerable sweet Ragas, and this is recommended by the author of Sangeeta Ratnakaram. But this was never the custom either with the ancients or with modern musicians. The ancient system was to make Ganam in the 12 concordant and branch Swarams with 22 Alakus omitting one Alaku each for 2 of those Swarams. Without understanding this ancient Tamil method, they have advocated 22 Srutis in the octave, and the names given by them to the Srutis make confusion worse confounded. Literature on music clearly proves that there was doubt as regards numbers and names of Srutis.

It is clearly found that they speak of 2 Alakus, 4 Alakus, and 6 Alakus in ancient times. This exactly corresponds to the Alaku Nilai found in the fractional and integral mathematical Tables of Tamilians (எண் சுவடி.)

It appears from the above that, according to the system of the ancient Tamilians, Swarams and Srutis were named after the numbers of their respective Alakus, which was clearly understood by all. For example they spoke of RI with 1 Alaku, $1\frac{1}{4}$ Alakus, $1\frac{1}{2}$ Alakus, $1\frac{3}{4}$ Alakus, 2 Alakus or 4 Alakus (thus having the term Alaku after the Sruti), or as 4 Alakus RI, $4\frac{1}{4}$ Alakus RI, $4\frac{1}{2}$ Alakus RI, $4\frac{3}{4}$ Alakus RI, 5 Alakus RI (thus placing the term Alaku before the name of the Sruti). This seems to be a very clear way of expressing the Swarasthanams and one which could be easily understood by all.

14. Examples showing the particular Srutis used in modern Ragas which follow the system of the ancient Tamilians.

(Karunamirtha Sagaram in Tamil Page 869—882.)

We made a few remarks about the Swarams, Srutis and very minute Srutis used in Isai-Tamil, sweeter than nectar, in which the ancient Tamilians were so highly proficient. We find that their excellence was quite in keeping with the efficiency they had attained in other sciences such as Anatomy, Physiology, Astronomy, Medicine and Philosophy. Music has also been developed in proportion as the inner meaning and calculations of other sciences had advanced.

We see that the ancient Tamilians, the Pandya sovereigns who ruled in South Madura and the scholars of the Tamil Sangams were efficient in Isai-Tamil, that they completely understood even the very minute Srutis used in music, and that they sang the praises of God in Pahs proportionate to the subtlety of those Srutis. We know that the several religious *puns* such as Thirugnanam, Thevaram and Thiruvachakam which are sung from the very ancient times and that several other religious *puns* anterior to that time are sung up to the present day in accordance with the rules of ancient Isai-Tamil.

It is a fact that we are singing only the ancient *puns* and Ragas according to the ancient methods and we are singing nothing new. But we have reached the stage where the names of these Puns and Ragas have been completely changed by strangers, nay, the Tamilians are accused of ignorance of music! Such is the times!

It is said that Narada gave the Suvadi treating about the minuteness of Ragas to Theagarajayar, who lived at Tiruvadi, as a great devotee of Rama, about 60 years ago. But ancient works on Isai-Tamil speak of Narada as Yal-asirian. Though we see in his Keertanams the Srutis of the four Palais of the ancient Tamilians, as modern musicians have no idea how the ancient Puns were chanted, we had to quote a few of his Keertanams here for demonstration. The result of our researches on Puns as well as on Ragas and Srutis will be published later on.

My opinions may appear very strange to many advocates of 22 Srutis who live in this age when there is a great doubt about Srutis. However, I have stated them hoping perhaps it might be of some use to unbiassed musicians who are close observers.

I have to state again and again that the ancients divided the octave into 12 half Swarams by the principle of concordant and branch Swarams (SA-PA and SA-MA systems), then divided them into 24 Alakus according to the system of Vattapalai and made their Ganam with 2 Alakus less.

The Tables have been shown separately according to the system in use among the ancient Tamilians. Table 5 gives some of the Desika Ragas and Hindustani Ragas which have different Swarams in Arohanam and Avarohanam. Tables 1, 2, 3 and 4 give some of the Marga Ragas which satisfy the rules of South Indian music.

We have already noticed that the Tamilians were highly proficient in Isai-Tamil, that they were competent to use and discriminate between the minutest Srutis, and that the Ragas of the present day date from very ancient times though their names have been mutilated in many ways.

We see that dealers in grains and miscellaneous articles and other merchants have been using uniform measures like one measure, $\frac{1}{2}$ a measure, $\frac{1}{4}$ of a measure, $\frac{1}{8}$ of a measure and $\frac{1}{16}$ of a measure and weights like 1 palam, $\frac{1}{2}$ a palam, $\frac{1}{4}$ of a palam, $\frac{1}{8}$ of a palam and $\frac{1}{16}$ of a palam, and many such devices so that there may be no difficulty in their dealings with others, and such devices exist even at present.

In the same manner in music also the different measurements such as Ayapalai, Vattapalai, Thirikonapalai and Chathurapalai have been used so that the Swarams which they use in any music might be easily classified.

The term '*Palai*' means "that which is divided" and "one of the sweet tastes of music". This shows they had four divisions to suit the different sounds of the *puns* sung.

Of these, Ayapalai admits of ganam in the 12 Swarams of a Sthayi derived by the SA-PA and the SA-MA systems.

Vattapalai consists of 24 Srutis with 2 Alakus for each of the 12 Swarams of the Sthayi, but the ganam is made with an Alaku less in each of the two concordant or branch Swarams like Vilari and Kaikilai. The other Swarams belong to Ayapalai.

Thirikonapalai admits of ganam with half the Alakus of the concordant and branch Swarams of Vattapalai. The other Swarams are those of Ayapalai.

Chathurapalai admits of ganam with quarter Alaku Swarams of the Vattapalai series, in other words, it has very minute Srutis like $\frac{1}{4}$, $\frac{3}{4}$, $1\frac{1}{4}$ and $1\frac{3}{4}$. The other Swarams are those of Ayapalai. By this, we do not mean that all Swarams should lose their original position in the octave and sound with the minutest Srutis. But only the two Swarams which are Jeevaswarams in Arohanam and Avarohanam should admit minute Srutis with 1 Alaku, $\frac{1}{2}$ Alaku, $\frac{1}{4}$ Alaku and so on.

The Tables 1, 2, 3 and 4 give the Ragas with Srutis according to the 4 Palais given above. They are easily understood. Of these

the first Table gives the Ragas where the 12 half Swarams of Ayapalai are used,

the second Table gives those where the quarter Swarams of Vattapalai are also used,

the third gives those Ragas where the $\frac{1}{8}$ Srutis of Thirikonapalai also occur along with other Swarams,

the fourth gives those Ragas where the $\frac{1}{16}$ Srutis of Chathurapalai are used along with other Swarams.

and the fifth contains the Ragas which contain Srutis mixed with Desikam in Karnatic music and Hindustani music.

The Ragas given in Table 1 are the ones most commonly in use in Karnatic music. These are sung in half Swarams only in Ayapalai by the ancient Tamilians. These occur with 2, 4 or 6 Alakus in the 12 Rasis. They stand in the relation of Vadi and Samvadi Swarams or concordant and branch Swarams to one another.

We may notice that as a rule, RI with 2 Alakus is followed by DHA with 2 Alakus, RI with 4 Alakus by DHA with 4, GA with 4 Alakus by NI with 4, and GA with 6 Alakus is followed by NI with 6.

The corresponding Arohana and Avarohana Swarams are found in the Table on page 55. The Ragam should proceed strictly by the Swarams in Arohanam and Avarohanam and according to the Alakus given in the Table. This is Margam. We shall give in book II some of the rules relating to this.

Table I showing the Ragas of Ayapalai.

The Ragas of Ayapalai in the 12 half Srutis.

No.	Kartha.	Ragam.	SA	RI 1	2	3	4	5	6	7	GA 2	3	4	5	6	7	MA 2	3	4	5	PA	DHA 1	2	3	4	5	6	7	NI 2	3	4	5	6	7	SA
1	Dhirasankarabaranam.	... ...	2				4								6		2				2				4								6		
2	Harikambothi ...	... ...	2				4								6		2				2				4						4				
3	Kharakarappiriya ...	... ...	2				4						4				2				2				4						4				
4	Natapyravi ...	... ...	2				4						4				2				2		2								4				
5	Hanumaththodi ...	... ...	2		2								4				2				2		2								4				
6	Mechakalyani ...	... ...	2				4								6				4		2				4								6		
7	Mayamalavam ...	... ...	2		2										6		2				2		2										6		
8	Chakravaham ...	... ...	2		2										6		2				2				4						4				
9	Dhirasankarabaranam	Pankala	2				4								6		2				2				0								6		
10	Kanakayabhooshani...	Kankayapooshani.	2						6						6		2				2		2										6		
11	Vahatheesvari ...	Sayanattai ...	2						6						6		2				2				4						4				
12	Vanaspathi	Vanaspathi ...	2		2						2						2				2				4						4				
13	Harikambothi ...	Kunthalavarali ...	2				0								0		2				2				4						4				
14	Natapyravi	Jayantha Sri ...	2				0						4				2				2		2								4				
15	Dhirasankarabaranam.	Karudathoni ...	2				4								6		2				2				4								6		
16	Karakarapiriya ...	Salakhapyravi ...	2				4						4				2				2				4						4				
17	Harikambothi ...	Kokilathoni ...	2				4								6		2				2				4						4				
18	Dhirasankarabaranam.	Kolakalam ...	2				4								6		2				2				4								6		
19	Harikambothi ...	Sinthukannada ...	2				4								6		2				2				4						4				
20	Dhirasankarabaranam.	Sinthumanthari...	2				4								6		2				2				4								6		

Table I showing the Ragas of Ayapalai.

No.	RAGAMS.	AROHANAM.	AVAROHANAM.
1	Dhirasankaraparanam.	s r g m p d n s ...	... s n d p m g r s
2	Harikambothi	s r g m p d n s ...	... s n d p m g r s
3	Karakarappiriya ...	s r g m p d n s ...	... s n d p m g r s
4	Natapyravi	s r g m p d n s ...	... s n d p m g r s
5	Hanumathodi	s r g m p d n s ...	... s n d p m g r s
6	Mechakalyani	s r g m p d n s ...	... s n d p m g r s
7	Mayamalavam ...	s r g m p d n s ...	... s n d p m g r s
8	Sakravaham	s r g m p d n s ...	... s n d p m g r s
9	Pankala	s r g m p n p s ...	... s n p m r g r s
10	Kankayabhoosani ...	s r g m p d n s ...	... s n d p m g r s
11	Sayanattai	s r g m p m p s ...	... s n d n p m r s
12	Vanaspathi	s r g m p d n s ...	... s n d p m g r s
13	Kunthalavarali ...	s m p d n d s ...	... s n d p m s
14	Jayantha Sri	s g m d n s ...	... s n d m p m g s
15	Karudathoni	s r g m p d n s ...	... s d p g r s
16	Salakapyravi	s r m p d s ...	... s n d p m g r s
17	Kokilathoni	s r g m d n d s ...	... s n d n p m g r s
18	Kolakalam	s p m g m p d n s	... s n d p m g r s
19	Sinthukannada ...	s m g m r g m p s	... s n d p m g r s
20	Sinthumanthari ...	s r g m p s ...	... s n d p g m d p m r s

Table II Ragas of Vattapalai.

The Ragas of Vattapali in the 24 quarter Srutis.

No.	Kartha.	Ragam.	SA	RI							GA						MA				PA	DHA							NI						SA
				1	2	3	4	5	6	7	2	3	4	5	6	7	2	3	4	5		1	2	3	4	5	6	7	2	3	4	5	6	7	
1	Dhirasankarabaranam.	Piyakadai ...	2				4								6			3			2				4							5			
2	Mayamalavam ...	Savari	2	1										5			2				2	1										5			
3	Neethimathi	Kaikavesi ...	2				4						4							5	2						6							7	
4	Harikambothi ...	Sahana	2				4									7	2				2				4							5			
5	Bavapriya	Bavapriya ...	2	1								3½							4½		2	1								3½					
6	Dhirasankarabaranam.	Devagandhari ...	2				4¾							5	*		2				2				4¾							5	*		

Table II. Ragas of Vattapalai.

This is the system of Ganam by which the ancient Tamilians divided each of the Rasis into 2 Alakus according to the Vattapalai system thus obtaining 24 Srutis in the octave and made Ganam with one Alaku less in two of the Rasis which are related as concordant or branch.

We see here that some of the Swarams of Ayapalai with even number of Alakus such as 2, 4 and 6 occur as Swarams with odd numbers of Alakus. For example, Saveri and Bhavapriya have Ri_1 and Dha_1 instead of Ri and Dha with 2 Alakus. In the same manner Saveri has Ni_3 and Ga_3 in place of Ni_4 and Ga_4. But in Bhavapriya Ga_5 and Ni_5 are a little sharper. In Devagandhari Ga and Ni have 5 Alakus each but Ri and Dha have $4\frac{3}{4}$ Alakus. Sahana has Ga_7 and Ni_7. Kaikavasi has the 5th Alaku of Ma and the 7th Alaku of Ni. Biakatai has Ma_3 and Ni_5. We find that all the above have odd Srutis in the 24 Srutis of Vattapalai but have even Swarams according to those of Ayapalai.

Devagandari has Ga and Ni with 6 Alakus very rarely. They may be found to have different Srutis while being sung. The Arohanams and Avarohanams of Ragas are given below.

No.	Ragams.	Arohanam.	Avarohanam.
1	Byakadai	s g r g m p d p s ...	s n d p m g r s
2	Saveri...	s r m p d s...	s n d p m g r s
3	Kaikavesi	s r g m p d n s	s n p m g r s
4	Sahana	s r g m p m d n s ...	s n s d p m ga m r s
5	Bhavapriya	s r g m p d n s... ...	s n d p m g r s
6	Devagandhari ...	s r m p d s	s n d p m g r s

Table III. Ragas of Thirikonapalai.

The Ragas sung with 48 one-eighth Srutis according to the system of Thirikonapalai.

Number.	Kartha.	Ragam.	SA	RI							GA						MA				PA	DHA							NI						SA
				1	2	3	4	5	6	7	2	3	4	5	6	7	2	3	4	5		1	2	3	4	5	6	7	2	3	4	5	6	7	
1	**Dhirasankaraparanam.**	Sankarabaranam..	2				4½								6		2				2				4½								6		
2	**Hanumaththodi** ...	Thodi	2		2							3½					2				0		2							3½					
3	Do.	Thanniasi ...	2		2								4½				2				2		2								4½				
4	**Bavappiriya**	Bavappiriya ...	2	1								3½							4½		2	1								3½					
5	**Thanuka**	Thanuka... ...	2		2							3½					2				2		2										6		
6	**Salanattai**	Nattai	2						6½						6		2				2						6						6½		
7	**Mayamalavam** ...	Phouli	2		2										6½		0				2		2										6½		
8	**Harikambothi** ...	Palahamsa ...	2				4½								6		2				2				4½						4				
9	**Karakarapiriya** ...	Aboki	2				4						4½				2				0				4							0			
10	**Shunmugappiriya** ...	Shunmugappiriya	2				4					3½							4½		2		2							3½					
11	**Kamavarthani** ...	Kamavarthani ...	2		2										6				4½		2		2										6		
12	**Harikambothi** ...	Nattaikurinji ...	2				4½								6		2				2				4						4½				
13	**Karakarapiriya** ...	Sriranjini ...	2				4						4½				2				0				4						4½				
14	**Dhirasankaraparanam**	Hamsadhoni ...	2				4½								6½		0				2				0								6½		
15	**Harikambothi** ...	Mohanam ...	2				4½								6½		0				2				4½						0				

Table III. Ragas of Thirikonapalai.

The Swarams in the above Table with an even number of Alakus such as 2, 4 and 6 are those of Ayapalai. But we see some of those Swarams either with half an Alaku more or half an Alaku less, such as $4+\frac{1}{2}=4\frac{1}{2}$ and $4-\frac{1}{2}=3\frac{1}{2}$. The Ri and Dha of Sankarabharanam have $4\frac{1}{2}$ Alakus each, while the other Swarams are Suddha. The Ga and Ni in Thodi have $3\frac{1}{2}$ Alakus each. The Ga and Ni of Thanyasi have $4\frac{1}{2}$. In the Natai Ragam (about whose Srutis there was such a discussion at the first meeting of the Tanjore Mahajana Sabha and at which no definite conclusion was arrived at) the Ri and Ni have $6\frac{1}{2}$ Alakus. In Hamsadoni the Ga and Ni have $6\frac{1}{2}$ Alakus. In the same way the Table will show that Ma has $4\frac{1}{2}$ and Ri, Ga, Dha and Ni $6\frac{1}{2}$ Alakus each. The other Swarams are those of Ayapalai.

This is used as Thirikonapalai by the ancient Tamilians. These Ragas have been in use from the ancient times as seen from the Puns and Keertanams found in ancient Isai-Tamil.

The Arohanams and Avarohanams of Ragas are given in the following Table.

No.	Ragams.	Arohanam.	Avarohanam.
1	Sankarabharanam ...	s r g m p d n s	s n d p m g r s
2	Thodi	s r g m d n s	s n d m g r s
3	Thannyasi	s g m p n s	s n d p m g r s
4	Dhenuka	s r g m p d n s	s n d p m g r s
5	Nattai	s r g m p d n s	s n p m r s
6	Bhouli	s r g p d s	s n d p g r s
7	Balahamsa	s r m p d s	s n d p m r m g s
8	Apohi	s r g m d s	s d m g r s
9	Shanmukhapriya ...	s r g m p d n s	s n d p m g r s
10	Kamavardhini ...	s r g m p d n s	s n d p m g r s
11	Nattaikurinji	s r g m n d n p d n s...	s n d m g s
12	Sriranjeni	s r g m d n s	s n d m g r s
13	Hamsadhoni ...	s r g p n s	s n p g r s
14	Mohanam	s r g p d s	s d p g r s

Table IV. Ragas of Chathurapalai.

The Ragas sung with 96 one-sixteenth Srutis according to the system of Chathurapalai.

Number.	Kartha.	Ragam.	Sa	Ri							Ga						Ma				Pa	Dha							Ni						Sa
				1	2	3	4	5	6	7	2	3	4	5	6	7	2	3	4	5		1	2	3	4	5	6	7	2	3	4	5	6	7	
1	Karakarapiriya.	Madhimavathi...	2				$4\frac{3}{4}$						0				2				2				0						$4\frac{3}{4}$				
2	,, ...	Nayaki ...	2				4					$3\frac{3}{4}$					2				2				4					$3\frac{3}{4}$					
3	Thirasankarabaranam.	Dhevaganthari.	2				$4\frac{3}{4}$							5	*		2				2				$4\frac{3}{4}$							5	*		
4	,, ...	Arabi ...	2				$4\frac{1}{4}$								6		2				2				$4\frac{1}{4}$								6		
5	,, ...	Purnachandrigi	2				$4\frac{1}{4}$								6		2				2				$4\frac{1}{4}$								6		
6	,, ...	Kakanakuthukalam.	2				$4\frac{1}{4}$								6		2				2				4								6		
7	Harikambothi...	Sanjuriti ...	2				$4\frac{1}{4}$								6		2				2				$4\frac{1}{4}$						4				
8	,, ...	Navarasakannada	2				4								6		2				2				4					$3\frac{3}{4}$					
9	,, ...	Nagaswarawali	2				0								6		2				2				$4\frac{1}{4}$						0				
10	Hanumaththodi	Himanki ...	2		2							$3\frac{3}{4}$					2				2		2							$3\frac{3}{4}$					
11	Karakarapiriya.	Kanada ...	2				4						$4\frac{3}{4}$				2				2				4						$4\frac{3}{4}$				

Table IV. Ragas of Chathurapalai.

When we examine the above Ragas we find that with the exception of ¼ and ¾ Swarams the rest belong to Ayapalai. Ri and Dha have ¼ or ¾ Alaku added on to the 4 Alakus, and Ga and Ni have 3¾ and 4¾ Alakus. The other Swarams are the half Swarams of Ayapalai.

But in Devagandari the Ga and Ni have one Alaku less and so have only 5. This system of lessening an Alaku for Ga and Ni by the Vattapalai, and adding a ¼ or ¾ Alaku for the same by Chathurapalai adds a peculiar charm to the ganam. Lessening an Alaku for Ga and Ni (Vattapalai) and adding a ¼ or ¾ Alaku for Ri and Dha (Chathurapalai) according to the different systems is the cause of the sweetness of the Ragas.

If we notice Devagandari and Arabi which generate from Dheerasankarabaranam and which have the same Arohanam and Avarohanam (Sa Ri Ma Pa Dha Sa and Sa Ni Dha Pa Ma Ga Ri Sa), the Ri and Dha in Devagandari have 4¾ Alakus each while the same occur in Arabi with 4¼ Alakus. Again, Ga and Ni have one Alaku less or 5 according to Vattapalai in Devagandari but in Arabi Ga with 6 Alakus or Anthara Ga and Ni with 6 Alakus or Kakali Ni occur.

So this system with one Alaku less than that of Ayapalai (which is Vattapalai) and ¼ an Alaku less than that of Ayapalai (which is Thirikonapalai) and ¼ Alaku more than that of Ayapalai (which is Thirikonapalai) has been in use from very ancient times.

These sharp Swarams, we know, are played as Gamakams in the 12 frets of the Veena. The ancient Tamilians have called Gamakam by the name 'Padalamutham' or 'the nectar of music' or the most charming parts in a melody. There is reason to think that others applied the name Padalamutham to the Jeeva Swarams.

For, in the above Table, Ri and Dha are sharper by ¼ or ¾ Alaku. It is these sharp Swarams that are the very life of the particular Ragas. In the same manner the Ri Dha Ga Ni and Ma which are made sharp in each of the Ragas from the Jeevaswarams.

We find from the Table that Ri and Dha in Sankarabaranam and Ga and Ni in Thodi are mentioned as Jeevaswarams. There are reasons why these particular Swarams should be Jeevaswarams. There is also a method for determining the Jeevaswarams in each Ragam. They will be given in detail in Book II. The Arohanams and Avarohanams of Ragas are given in the Table below.

No.	Ragams.	Arohanam.	Avarohanam.
1	Madhimavathi ...	s r m p n s	s n p m r s
2	Nayaki	s r m p d n d p s	s n s d p m r g r s
3	Dhevaganthari ...	s r m p d s	s n d p m g r s
4	Arabi	s r m p d s	s n d p m g r s
5	Poornachandrigai ...	s r g m p d p s...	s n p d p m g m r s
6	Kakânakuthukalam ...	s r m d n g p s...	s n d p m g r s
7	Sanjuriti ...	d s r g m p d n	d p m g r s n d p
8	Navarasakannada ...	s g m p s	s n d m g r s
9	Nagaswarali	s g m p d s	s d p m g s
10	Himangi	s r g m p d n d s	s n p d m g r s
11	Kanada	s r g m p m d n s... ...	s n p m n d p m g m r s

Table V. Some Desika Ragas and Hindustani Ragas.

Number.	Kartha.	The opening words of songs.	SA	RI							GA						MA				PA	DHA							NI						SA
				1	2	3	4	5	6	7	2	3	4	5	6	7	2	3	4	5		1	2	3	4	5	6	7	2	3	4	5	6	7	
1	Saranga	Nee vadala kana ...	2				4								6		2		4		2				4								6		
2	Pyak	Mangalam Sleika ...	2				4								6		2		4		2				4						4		6		
3	Thesiga Kalyani ...	Singara vana kanitha...	2				4								6		2		4		2				4								6		
4	Gaupi	Dheem na thera dheem	2				4						4				2				2		2		4						4				
5	Bhairavi	Koluvai yunadha ...	2				4						4				2				2		2		4						4				
6	Anantha Bhairavi...	Atharamunai alhall ..	2				4						4				2				2		2		4						4				
7	Kaumbethi... ...	Eppadium pavikalai ...	2				4								6		2				2				4						4		6		
8	Adana	Pala kanakamaya ...	2				4								6		2				2				4						4		6		
9	Muhari	Ennaod kirupa kalkuno	2				4						4				2				2		2		4						4				
10	Pyahak	Savalisurattha Paramgi	2				4								6		2		4		2				4						4		6		
11	Ameerakalyani ...	Thurasa pola pola ...	2				4								6		2		4		2				4								6		
12	Kamas	Nathiyakinari pasiyan.	2				4								6		2				2		2		4						4		6		
13	Maunt	Mee abarathikaravidow	2				4								6		2				2				4						4		6		
14		Kona daya karathutha	2				4								6		2				2				4						4		6		
15	Hindustani Kanada	Soapara mesarasasani	2				4						4	5			2				2				4						4	5			

Table V. Some Desika Ragas and Hindustani Ragas.

We find from the above Table that Ragas have the 12 half Swarams of Ayapali but the fixed rule is that a Swaram which has a particular number of Alakus in Arohanam should have the same in Avarohanam also. This is Margam.

Sometimes a Swaram or two may be omitted or their order changed either in Arohanam or Avarohanam. But the number of Alakus should never be changed.

For example, a Ri with 4 Alaku should never be changed either in Arohanam or Avarohanam into one with 2 or 6 Alakus. The same rule applies to GA MA DHA and Ni. If they so occur, they infringe one of the fixed rules of South Indian music or Margam. This infringement of rules is called Desikam. No doubt these Desika Ragas are very pleasant as the mixture of sweetmeats like Boondhi and Ladu with salted mango or salted lemon which add flavour to the sweetness. But this can never be compared to the Ganam made strictly in accordance with the rules of Karnatic Music, which independently by itself has the power of charming even elephants and inducing cobras to spread their hood and dance. So we have not dealt with Desikam to any extent. I think what I have already given about Desikam in the first part is enough. The following Table gives the Arohanam and Avarohanam of Desika Ragas.

We notice in Table IV that in the system of Chathurapalai, in the Ragam Kanada, GA and NI had $4\frac{3}{4}$ Alakus each. When the same Ragam is sung as Hindustani, the NI and GA have 5 Alakus sometimes and even 4 Alakus at other times, while the other Swarams resemble those of the Karnatic Kanada. I am not able to give more examples of Hindustani Ragas as I am not well acquainted with them.

Again, if we notice Hindustani Ragas, we find that each of the Swarams in particular Ragas occurs continuously with one or more Swarams, indicating the Swarams pertaining to that Ragam and thus makes the Sancharam in Arohanam and Avarohanam. It is the custom to indicate the top Swarams while making Sancharam in the lower Swarams in Arohanam and *vice versa*. These are mostly the 12 half Swarams of Ayapalai. A few of the 24 Srutis of Vattapalai also rarely occur as in Hindustani Kanada. Those who are well acquainted with Hindustani music should inquire into this and give us the result of their observations.

No.	RAGAMS.	AROHANAM.	AVAROHANAM.
1	Sarnga	s r g m p d n s...	s n d p m r g m r s
2	Piyake	s g m p d n s	s n d p m g r s
3	Dhesikakalyani ...	s r g m p d n s...	s n d p m g r s –
4	Kabi	s r g m p n s	s d n p m r g m r s
5	Bairavi	s r g m p d n s...	s n d p m g r s
6	Ananthabairavi ...	s g r g m p d p s n s...	s n d p m g r s
7	Kambothi	s r g m p d s	s n d p m g r s
8	Adana	s r m p nee s	s n da p d n d p m g r s
9	Muhari	s r m p d s	s n d p m g r s

☛ A few remarks on Ragas, some measurement as regards marking the Swarasthanam in a Yal, some quotations from Thevaram and Thiruvachakam in proof of the Ragas used in Isai-Tamil, some remarks and inscriptions as regards the Pandya sovereigns who were the patrons of Isai-Tamil and a few remarks of others as regards Karnatic music and the Tamil country will be given later on.

15. Some important points to be noted.

In the first part of the book, I have stated that many scholars at the present day hold that the present space occupied by the Indian Ocean was originally an extensive land portion, that it was the first Paradise of Man, that the inhabitants there belonged to the prehistoric period, that they were proficient in all learning. arts and handicrafts even as early as 22,000 years ago, and that when their habitation was submerged they escaped to the lands opposite them and settled there. I have also stated there, that the destroyed continent of Lemuria was called the province of Kumari, that the province was made up of seven big islands, that South Madura was its capital, that the Pandya kings hereditarily ruled there for generations, that the language spoken there was Tamil, that the language had attained very high efficiency being called the Muttamil made up of Iyal, Isai and Natakam, that a distinguished Tamil Sangam was organised there 13,000 years ago and was carried on for 4,400 years being patronisd by eminent scholars and that while Lemuria was submerged *i. e.* 8000 years ago (as stated in the preface to Tholkaupiam) the ancient and eminent Tamil work known as Tholkaupiam was placed for approval before Athankotasan, one of the distinguished disciples of Ahatya, who flourishd in the reign of Nilantharuthiruvil Pandya, the Victorious, who ruled in South Madura or Lemuria. We have also observed how Tamil was a language of great antiquity, how music, which was one of the *amsams* of Tamil, had attained eminence from the earliest times, how it was patronised by Rajas and noblemen, and how it deteriorated in later times so much so people say that the Tamilians are ignorant of music. However, the concensus of opinion of ancient literature is in favour of the fact that the Tamilians were great experts in music. We see how they derived the mother-Ragas and the Ragas which generate from them with the help of the half Swarams of Ayapalai, how they used 12000 such Ragas for 13,000 years from now, how they derived the four kinds of Yal from Vattapalai—Marutham, Kurinji, Neythal and Palai—and the four Jathis, Ahanilai, Puranilai, Arugial and Perugial, how they had 24 Srutis in the octave and made Ganam with 22 Alakus, lessening 2 Alakus in Vilari and Kaikilai. We have observed how they divided their Ganam into four Palais—Ayapalai, Vattapalai, Thirikonapalai and Chathurapalai, and called the music with 12 half Swarams Ayapalai, with 24 quarter Swarams, Vattapalai, 48 one-eighth minute Swarams, Thirikonapalai and 96 one-sixteenth minute Swarams, Chathurapalai.

The 12,000 ancient Isais and the *puns* composed to suit those Isais have not altogether gone out of use in the present day, but are only seen under different names.

We see these Isais are the peculiar heritage of the Tamilians of the southern part of India. So in order to prove practically that what the people call the modern

Karnatic music is only another name for the music of the four Palais of the ancient Tamilians. I have distinctly written about the system of four Palais. If all the Karnatic Ragas could be minutely examined in the light of the system of four Palais, and the results published in the form of a Table, it will be of immense use to those who learn music.

The same Swarams used in Ayapalai—12, by each of the SA-PA and SA-MA series—are now reckoned as $\frac{3}{2}$ for SA-PA and $\frac{4}{3}$ for SA-MA with the result that the Sthayi does not come to a perfect end but has a few cents more or less in the reckoning. To add to this, we have come to an advanced stage where the octave is said to contain only 22 Srutis. Not satisfied with this we have come to the strange times which derive 53 Srutis in the Sthayi! All the above theories are the result of a complete ignorance of the four Palais system of the Tamilians.

I am afraid that nobody has yet realised the efficiency which the ancient Tamilians had attained in Isai-Tamil. Many of the Karnatic musicians of the modern day accustomed to the minute Srutis as well as beginners in music have lost the minuteness of Karnatic music because they practise on instruments constructed with 12 Swarams. Even those who sang the minute Srutis to the accompaniment of a Yal have been unable to discriminate the Srutis which they used and gave it up in despair. In course of time, I am afraid, even the 12 main Swarams of Ayapalai may be lost in the region of doubt! I think that the reason for this deterioration was due to the difficulty of learning to play the instrument called the Yal. It will be to advantage, if Swarams could determined by the Ayapalai, the four great *puns* and the four Jathis by the Vattapalai, and the minuter Swarams by Thirikonapalai and Chathurapalai. The music of any nation in the world, speaking any language, may be noted down according to this system. I can also say boldly that no nation was so proficient in Isai-Tamil or music as the ancient Tamilians. We see from their four-Palais-system that the ancient Tamilians were well-advanced in many excellent arts and Sciences. We have reason to think these are degenerate days because the ancient Ragas and scholars who patronised *Muttamil* have disappeared now and the eminence of music has also been completely forgotten.

I have also given mathematical calculations by which the Swarams, Srutis and minute Srutis of the four-Palais-system can be noted. I have given Tables to show the different minute Srutis in different Ragas, and have practically demonstrated them by singing. I am prepared to make further demonstrations to those who desire to know more about it.

You see before you the Veena in which the Swarasthanams are marked according to the measurements and its divisions given in the Table. In addition to that I have compared the measurements of the 22 Srutis in the octave according to Sarnga Dev and those of the Swarams obtained according to the system of the ancient Tamilians. You see from the comparative statement, that, with the exception of the Athara SA and its octave, not one Sruti tallies with the corresponding Sruti as regards measurement. Just as all men of knowledge are agreed that if weights and meaures are uniform it will be advantageous to all the world so also they must agree that if there be a common standard for the Swarams used in the music of the whole world it will be of immense help. Such is the measurement of the Srutis obtained by the system of Ayapalai. Vattapalai, Thirikonapalai and Chathurapalai which might be used as the standard for all, and all music might be written in this system with a common notation which could be easily understood by all.

I sincerely believe that by this system all our doubts as regards Srutis will be cleared, the shallowness of the system of Dwavimsati Srutis exposed, and that all other difficulties will vanish.

Ye members of this august assembly who have come here to know and enquire about the Srutis of Indian music! Your Highness the Gaekwar who has organised this Sabha for the enquiry into, and establishment of, truth! I have placed before you the result of my poor researches just like a baby which grows bold before the beloved father. I earnestly request you to be partial to my shortcomings and to accept any good which you may find there.

KARUNAMIRTHA SAGARAM.

EXTRACT
FROM
THE FIRST BOOK
ON
Staff Notation for Indian Music.
PART III.

An essay on Staff Notation for Indian Music read before the All-India Music Conference held at Baroda under the kind patronage of His Highness the Gaekwar of Baroda (22nd March, 1916.)

BY

MARAGATHAVALLI AMMAL.

DAUGHTER OF

RAO SAHIB M. ABRAHAM PANDITHER,

KARUNANITHI MEDICAL HALL,

TANJORE.

(Second Edition.)

KARUNAMIRTHA SAGARAM

EXTRACT FROM THE FIRST BOOK ON SRUTIS.

An essay on Staff Notation for Indian Music read before the All-India Music Conference held at Baroda under the kind patronago of

His Highness the Gaekwar of Baroda,

22nd March 1916.

STAFF NOTATION FOR INDIAN MUSIC.

I make my deep obeisance to HIS HIGHNESS THE GAEKWAR and to HER HIGHNESS THE MAHARANI who have shown great interest in Indian Music by bringing together this large assembly of Vidwans from different parts.

To those members assembled here with a view to find out what would be the best kind of Notation for Indian music which would help people to study it easily, I tender my respects. I request the members of this august assembly to forgive my boldness in saying a few words before them, inexperienced as I am.

It is a matter for regret that Indian Music, which has been held in high esteem from ancient times, has, for the last 2000 years or so, degenerated owing to want of patronage; times have so changed that, at present, researches are being made about Srutis which are the basis of all music! This is something like trying to find out the Alphabet of a language which was once noted for its high style and eminent literature! But we hope the time has come for the regeneration of Indian Music seeing that such an eminent ruler like the Gaekwar has taken the matter in hand.

Given the particular Ri, the particular Ga, Ma, Dha or Ni which occur in a Ragam, professional musicians who have made it their life-work will easily understand the ramification of the Ragam and will be able to compose many Keertanams and Varnams in the same. When they commit them to writing, they group all the Swarams one after another, in the form of an ordinary language, without employing any musical measure or symbol.

Even clever musicians will not be able to make it out at times, so much so that its real meaning is completely lost to their successors. Sometimes they will merely mention the particular Thalam (time) of a piece of music without giving its parts which might cause endless doubts. So we see the necessity of clearing all these doubts by having a new method of Notation which might be useful to all. No doubt there are differences of opinion on this subject. I make bold to place before you my own humble opinion and request you to give it due consideration.

We are all agreed that a system of Notation easily understandable by all will be of great use to students of music. We should understand that the members of the Tamil Sangam which existed in South Madura eight thousand years ago and other musicians of that age used the 12 half-Swarams of Ayapalai obtained by the Sa-Pa and the Sa-Ma principles in their Ganam. The succession of the same 12 Swarams is now known among the renowned musicians of Europe as the chromatic scale under Equal Temperament. This is considered highly useful for purposes of harmony and modulation and modern western musical instruments like the Piano and the Harmonium are constructed on this principle. For over 2500 years, from the time of Pythagoras, controversy has been going on about the measurements of the 12 Swarams of an octave obtained while supposing Sa-Pa to be $\frac{2}{3}$ and Sa-Ma $\frac{3}{4}$. The celebrated Western musicians Haydn, Mozart and Beethoven, about 120 years ago, found out the advantage of Equal Temperament and the result was the dawn of a new era in music and the perfection of symphony. Since then Europe has advanced by leaps and bounds in instrumental as well as vocal music, parts being written for wind as well as percussion instruments. Many an Indian has advanced in European music so much so that one is able to interpret the music of the west as well as make original compositions in the same. We have seen how a piece of English Music composed by an Englishman at one end of the world when written in Staff notation is faithfully interpreted and reproduced by an Indian at the other end. We have seen the excellence of the English Staff notation. The signs which indicate the duration and the increasing or decreasing intensity of different notes, the signs to denote speed, expression, and pauses, the signs giving special directions to the performer as to where a piece of music ends or where it is repeated from, time-signatures and key-signatures, and a variety of abbreviations and embellishments are the distinguishing features of European music. So my humble opinion is that to reproduce those Indian Ragas where these 12 half Swarams only occur, the Staff notation of the west is quite enough. This notation is already known to many Indians constituting military bands, and other private bands, to Indian organists who play on the Organ or the Harmonium in

Christian churches. even to students of Indian music who play their Ragas on a Harmonium and to those students of the science of English Music. So it will be of advantage to put them down on the Staff. By so doing we should understand that those Ragas made up of the 12 half-Swarams of the Ayapalai only are capable of being thus transferred and played on the Harmonium or the Piano.

We should bear in mind two other points. In the first place, the bars should be so divided as to suit the different Thalams in use in India, and secondly, special signs should be given to indicate the minute Srutis over and above the 12 Swarams. Though these minute Srutis could not be reproduced on the piano or the Harmonium they might be of use to vocal musicians as well as players on instruments like the Yal or the Veena, the Violin and the Flute.

We may notice on pages 872—880 of Karunamirtha Sagaram that concordant Swarams in an octave like Ri, Dha, Ga, Ni and Ma Ni occur a little sharp sometimes. We have Ri not only with 2 Alakus but with $2\frac{1}{4}$, $2\frac{1}{2}$, $2\frac{3}{4}$, 3, $3\frac{1}{4}$, $3\frac{1}{2}$, and $3\frac{3}{4}$ Alakus also. So we may indicate the $\frac{1}{4}$, $\frac{1}{2}$, $\frac{3}{4}$, 1, $1\frac{1}{4}$, $1\frac{1}{2}$ and $1\frac{3}{4}$ by the numbers 1, 2, 3, 4, 5, 6, 7 respectively. These numerals tacked on to a Swaram will indicate what minuter Srutis they should add on. For example, Ri 4^2 and Dha 4^2 will mean that $4\frac{1}{2}$ Alakus are meant in each case. These occur in Sankaraparanam. But the Signs Ri 4^1 and Dha 4^1 will indicate $4\frac{1}{4}$ Alakus for the two Swarams. These occur in Ragas like Arabi, Poornachandrika and Chenchuruti. Ragas with minute Srutis such as these in Vattapalai, Thirikonapalai and Chathurapalai might be found in the Tables given. So, to conclude. then, I am of opinion that.

(1) The English Staff notation with certain modifications may be advantageously used for the Ragas composed of the 12 half Swarams of Ayapalai.

(2) Indicating the minuter Srutis by means of numerals from 1 to 7 will be of use to vocalists as well as players on instruments with the exception of the Harmonium and the Piano.

(3) Bars should be so divided as to suit the variety of Thalams in use in Indian music.

The truth of my statements may be clearly understood if you would kindly listen to the four Keertanams I am going to sing purely with the help of the English Staff notation. If the many Ragas of India could be so transposed to Staff notation with the help of experts and published throughout India, a uniform method of singing will prevail throughout the length and breadth of the land. Ragas will be saved from mutilation and will be enjoyed and studied correctly by every one interested in Indian Music. Ordinary Gramaphone or Polyphone records of Indian Music are heard with delight. If those who appreciate these songs could be enabled to have all excellent Indian songs in Staff notation, they will not only appreciate them but would feel inspired to study Indian Music. The Music of India will then be rapturously admired and studied all over the world.

I have given below the Staff notation for the Pallavis of four Keertanams to indicate the Swarams, the Srutis, and the minute Srutis that occur in the four *Palais* of Isai-Tamil (Sangeetham) (Ayappalai, Vattappalai, Thirikonapalai and Chathurapalai,) which obtained among the Tamilians of yore.

1 AYAPALAI RAGAM.

Ragam: Garudadoni. Athithalam. 8-4-4

2 VATTAPALAI RAGAM.

Ragam: Kaikavachi. Athithalam. 8-4-4

3 THIRIKONAPALAI RAGAM.

Ragam: Shunmugapiria. Athithalam. 8-4-4

4 CHATHURAPALAI RAGAM.

Ragam: Chenchuruti. Athithalam. 8-4-4

N. B.—The Srutis marked 1, 2, 3, 4, 5, 6 and 7 are used for the Veena and vocal music only. But some use the Srutis marked 1, 2, 3 and 4 for the given note on the Harmonium and in singing and those marked 5, 6 and 7 for the note immediately above. An indiscriminate use of this is likely to spoil the beauty and minuteness of Indian music.

There are many more important points in connection with Staff notation, but I have placed before you what I considered only very necessary at this stage. They will be added on in course of time.

I thank His Highness the Gaekwar and Her Highness the Maharani and the eminent musicians assembled here for patiently listening to me and request they will give this their due consideration.